The Christian Children's SONGBOOK

P9-BIX-631

contents

ISBN 0-634-02794-8

HAL•LEONARD®
CORPORATION

7777 W. BLUEMOUND RD. P.O. BOX 13819 MILWAUKEE, WI 53213

Visit Hal Leonard Online at
www.halleonard.com

Alive, Alive

Registration 4
Rhythm: Country or Fox Trot

Traditional

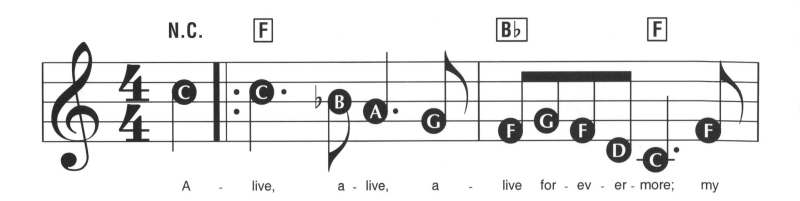

A - live, a - live, a - live for - ev - er - more; my

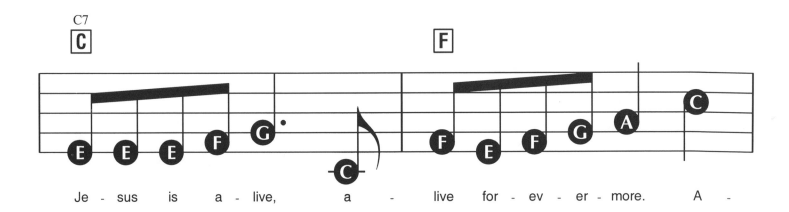

Je - sus is a - live, a - live for - ev - er - more. A -

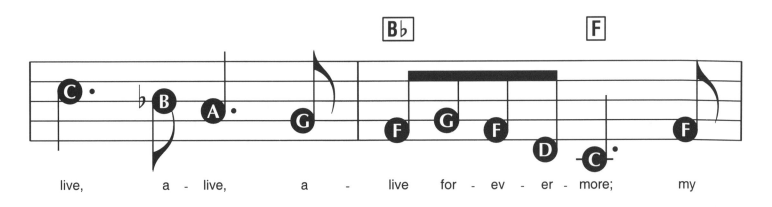

live, a - live, a - live for - ev - er - more; my

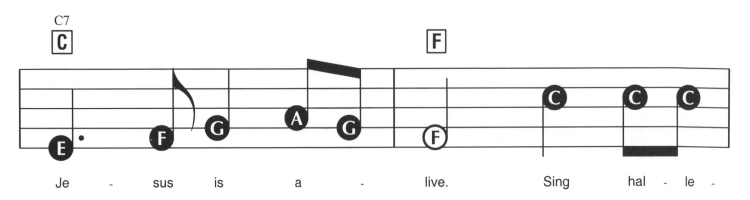

Je - sus is a - live. Sing hal - le -

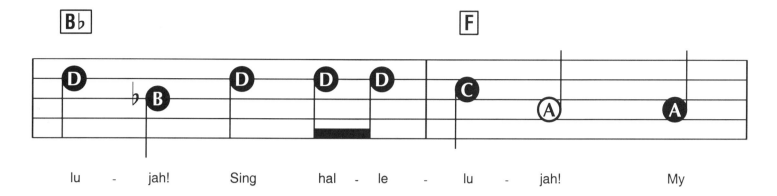

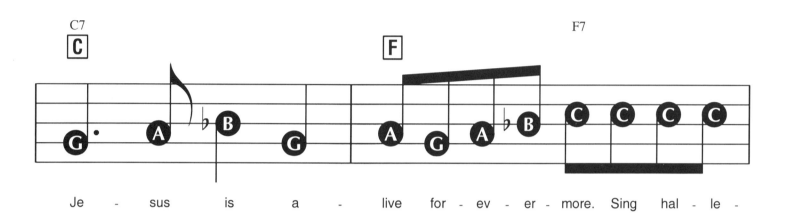

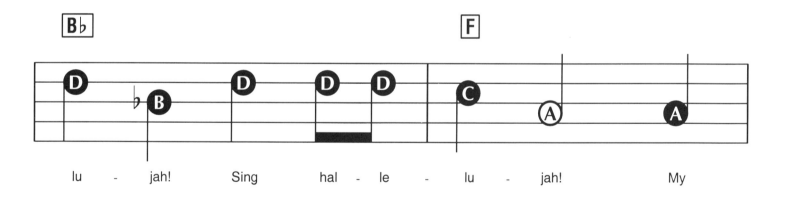

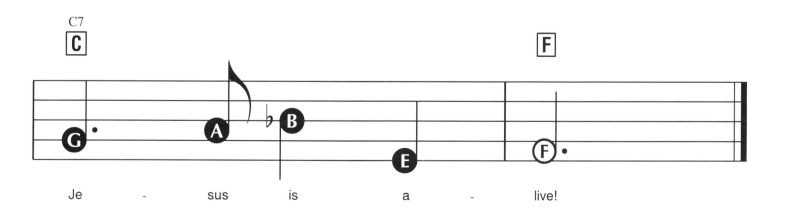

All God's Children Got Shoes

Registration 8
Rhythm: Gospel or March

Spiritual

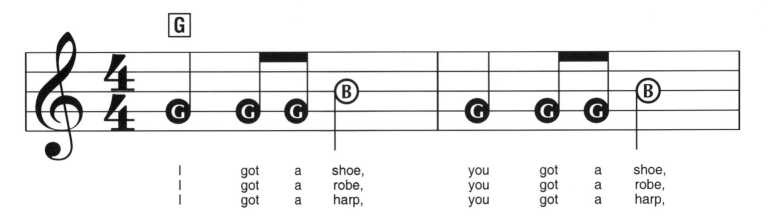

I got a shoe,   you got a shoe,
I got a robe,   you got a robe,
I got a harp,   you got a harp,

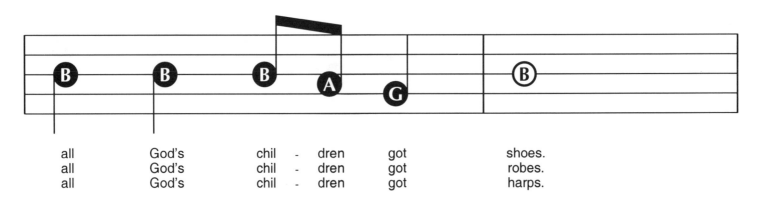

all God's chil - dren got shoes.
all God's chil - dren got robes.
all God's chil - dren got harps.

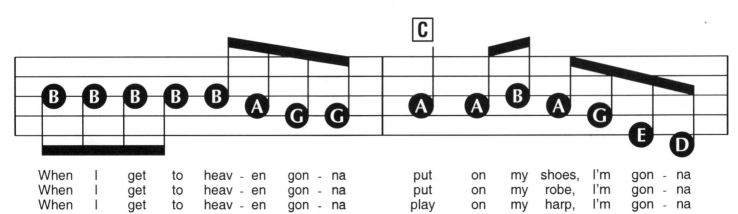

When I get to heav - en gon - na put on my shoes, I'm gon - na
When I get to heav - en gon - na put on my robe, I'm gon - na
When I get to heav - en gon - na play on my harp, I'm gon - na

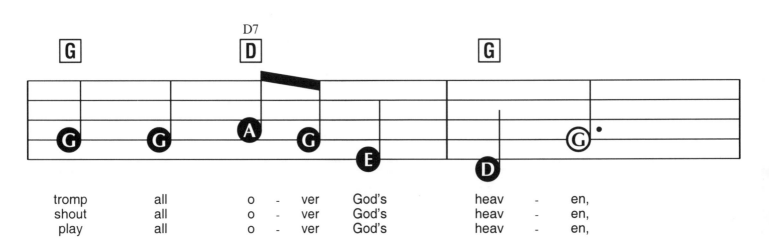

tromp all o - ver God's heav - en,
shout all o - ver God's heav - en,
play all o - ver God's heav - en,

All Night, All Day

Registration 2
Rhythm: Gospel or Fox Trot

Spiritual

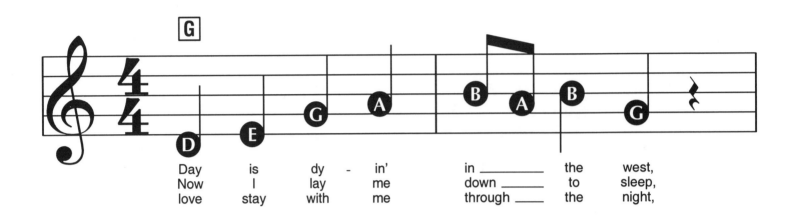

Day   is   dy - in'   in _____ the   west,
Now   I   lay   me   down _____ to   sleep,
love   stay   with   me   through ___ the   night,

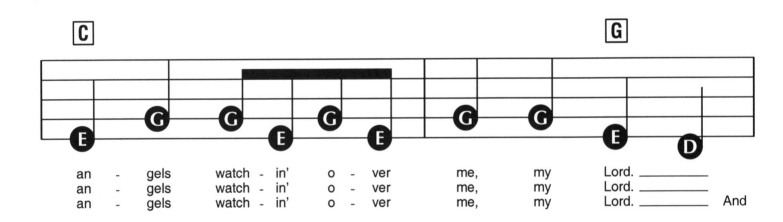

an - gels   watch - in'   o - ver   me,   my   Lord. _____
an - gels   watch - in'   o - ver   me,   my   Lord. _____
an - gels   watch - in'   o - ver   me,   my   Lord. _____ And

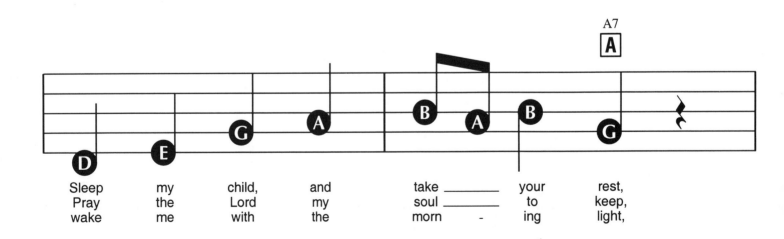

Sleep   my   child,   and   take _____ your   rest,
Pray   the   Lord   my   soul _____ to   keep,
wake   me   with   the   morn - ing   light,

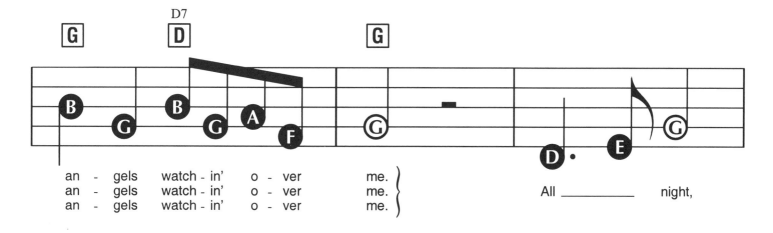

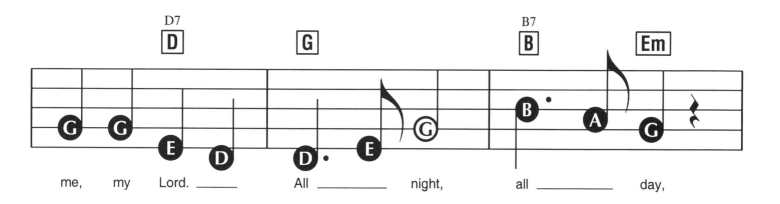

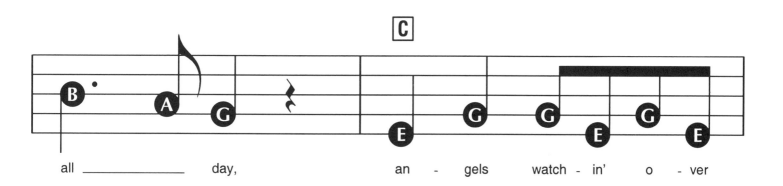

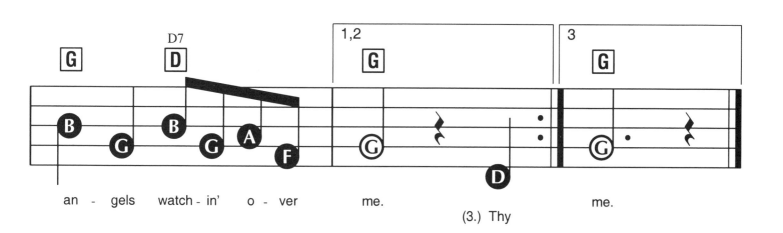

All Things Bright and Beautiful

Registration 8
Rhythm: Ballad or Country

Words by Cecil Frances Alexander
17th Century English Melody
Arranged by Martin Shaw

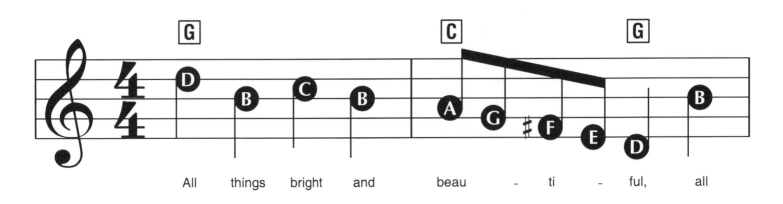

All things bright and beau - ti - ful, all

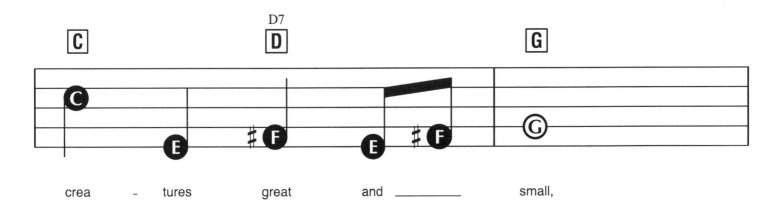

crea - tures great and _____ small,

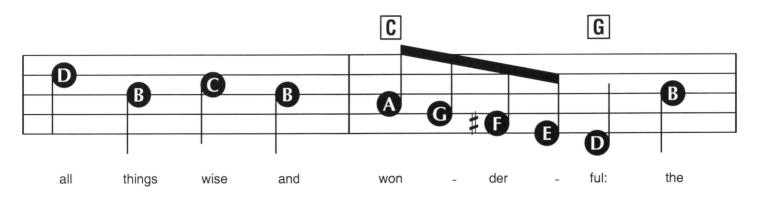

all things wise and won - der - ful: the

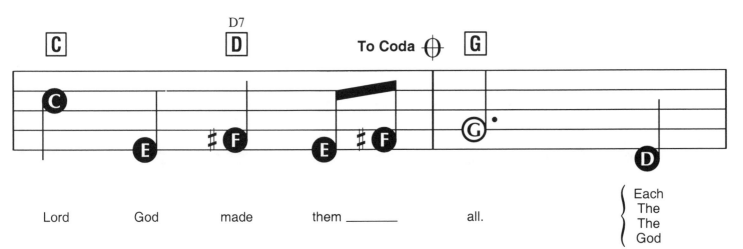

Lord God made them _____ all.

Each
The
The
God

Arky, Arky

Registration 9
Rhythm: March or Fox Trot

Traditional

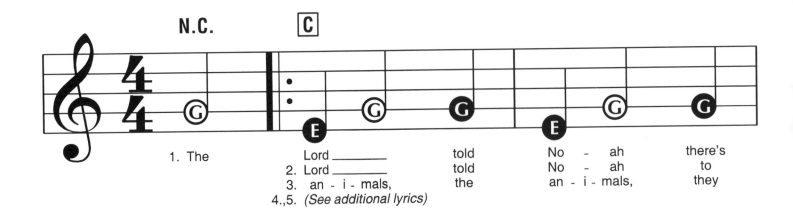

1. The Lord _____ told No - ah there's
2. Lord _____ told No - ah to
3. an - i - mals, the an - i - mals, they
4.,5. *(See additional lyrics)*

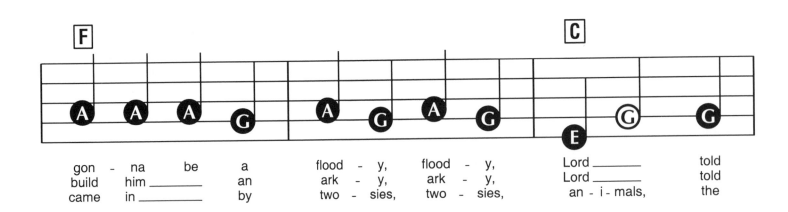

gon - na be a flood - y, flood - y, Lord _____ told
build him _____ an ark - y, ark - y, Lord _____ told
came in _____ by two - sies, two - sies, an - i - mals, the

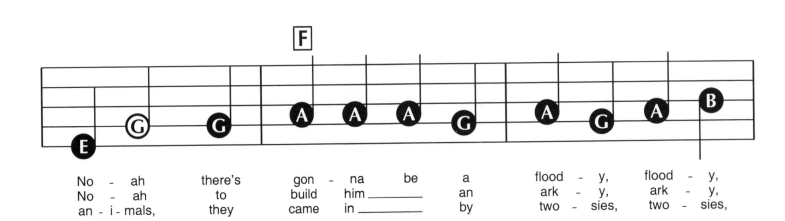

No - ah there's gon - na be a flood - y, flood - y,
No - ah to build him _____ an ark - y, ark - y,
an - i - mals, they came in _____ by two - sies, two - sies,

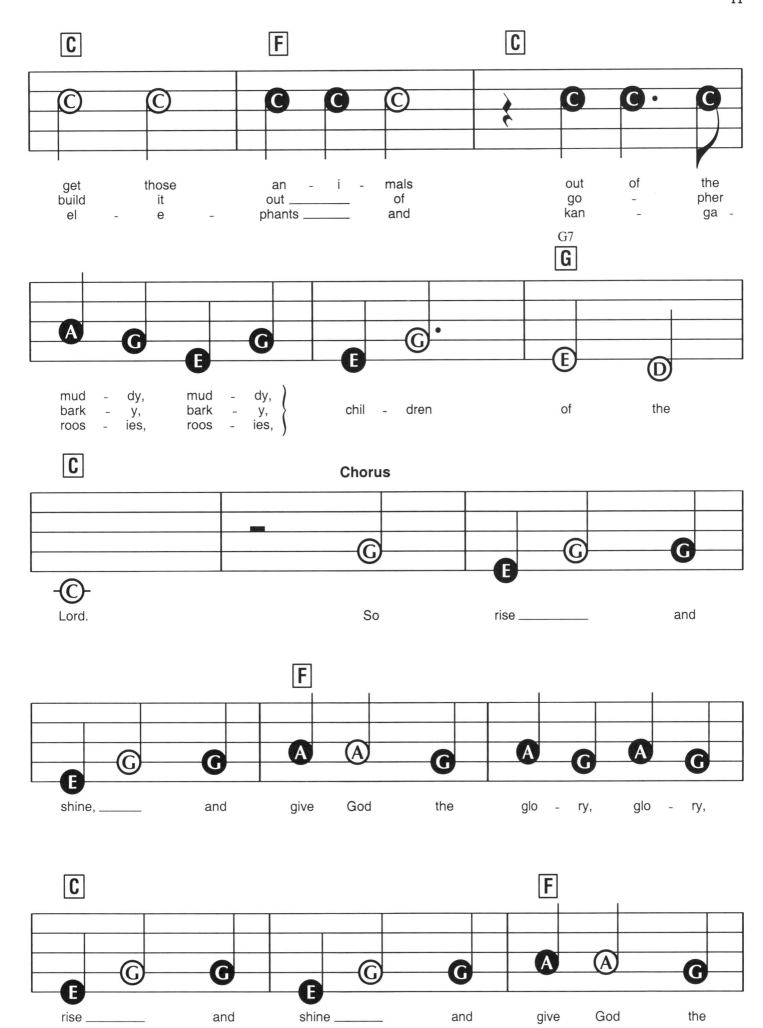

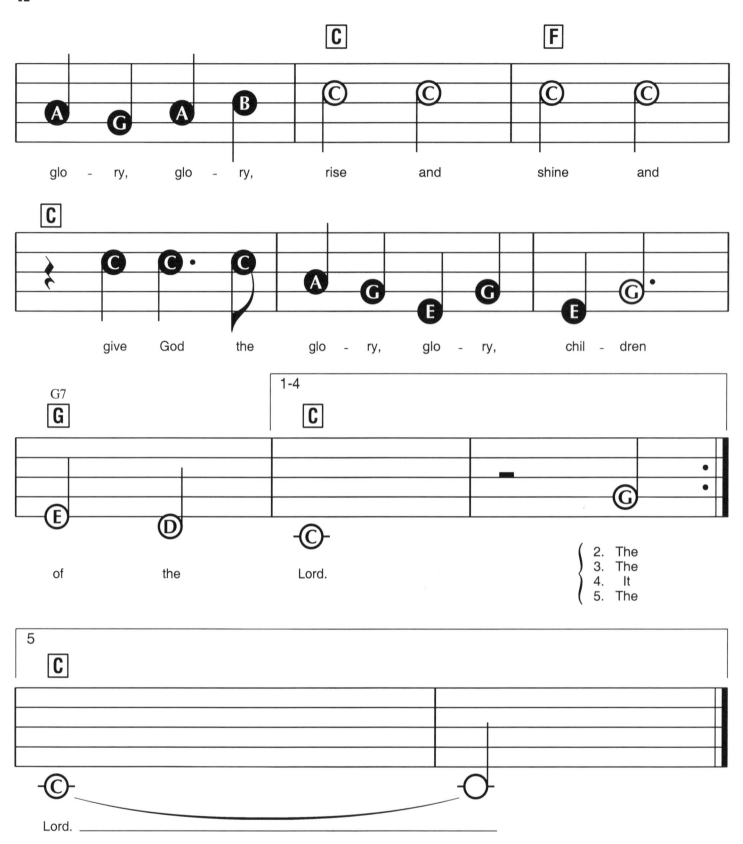

glo - ry, glo - ry, rise and shine and

give God the glo - ry, glo - ry, chil - dren

G7

1-4

of the Lord.

{ 2. The
3. The
4. It
5. The

5

Lord.

Additional Lyrics

4. It rained and poured for forty daysies, daysies,
   Rained and poured for forty daysies, daysies,
   Almost drove those animals crazies, crazies,
   Children of the Lord.
   Chorus

5. The sun came out and dried up the landy, landy,
   (Look, there's the sun!) It dried up the landy, landy,
   Everything was fine and dandy, dandy,
   Children of the Lord.
   Chorus

The B-I-B-L-E

Registration 8
Rhythm: Fox Trot

Traditional

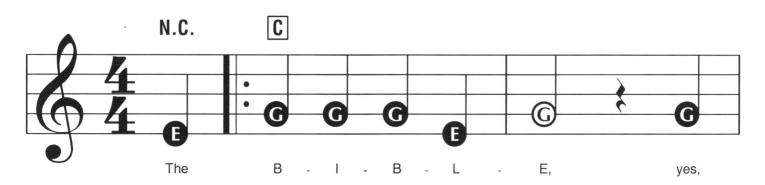

The B - I - B - L - E, yes,

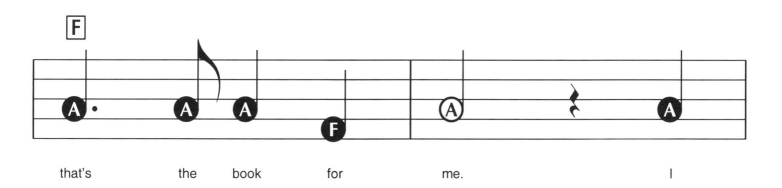

that's the book for me. I

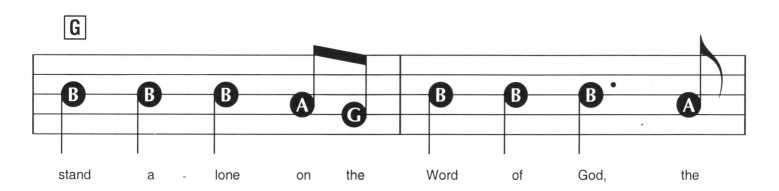

stand a - lone on the Word of God, the

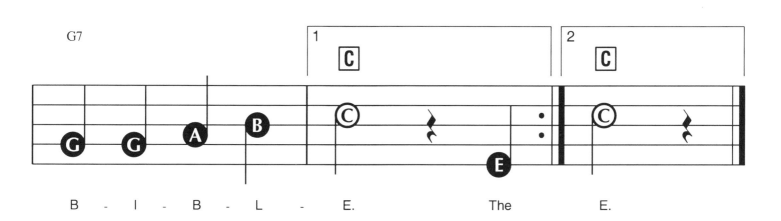

B - I - B - L - E. The E.

Come into His Presence

(Singing Alleluia)

Registration 8
Rhythm: Country or March

Unknown

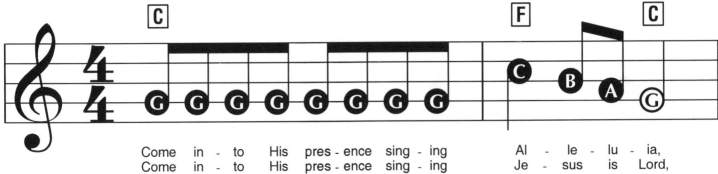

Come in - to His pres - ence sing - ing Al - le - lu - ia,
Come in - to His pres - ence sing - ing Je - sus is Lord,

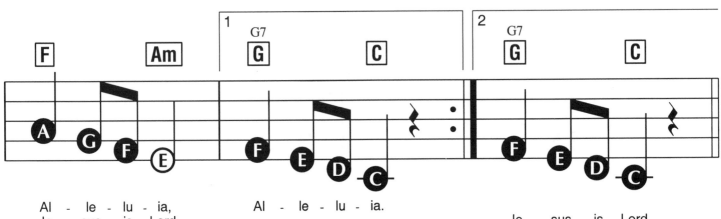

Al - le - lu - ia, Al - le - lu - ia.
Je - sus is Lord,

Je - sus is Lord.

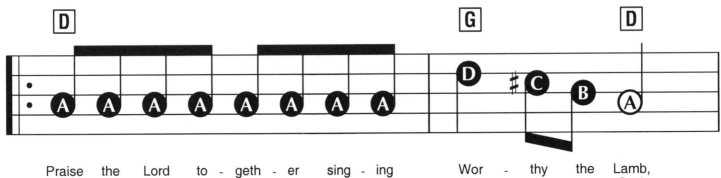

Praise the Lord to - geth - er sing - ing Wor - thy the Lamb,
Praise the Lord to - geth - er sing - ing Glor - ry to God,

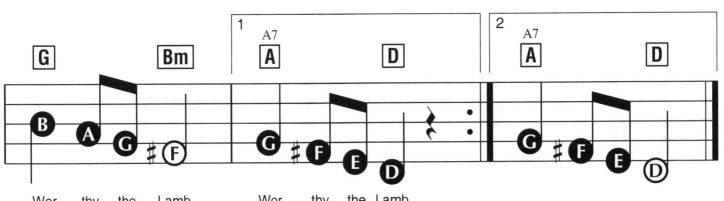

Wor - thy the Lamb, Wor - thy the Lamb.
Glo - ry to God,

Glo - ry to God.

Dare to Be a Daniel

Registration 2
Rhythm: March

Words and Music by
Philip P. Bliss

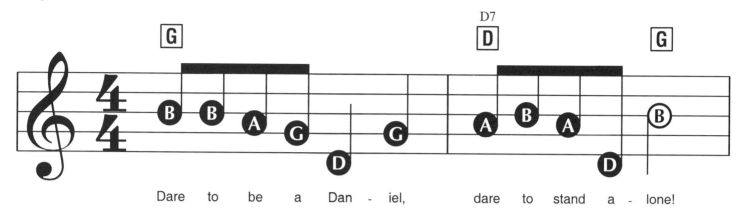

Dare to be a Dan - iel, dare to stand a - lone!

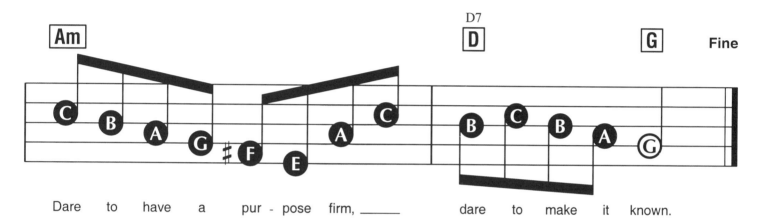

Dare to have a pur - pose firm, _____ dare to make it known.

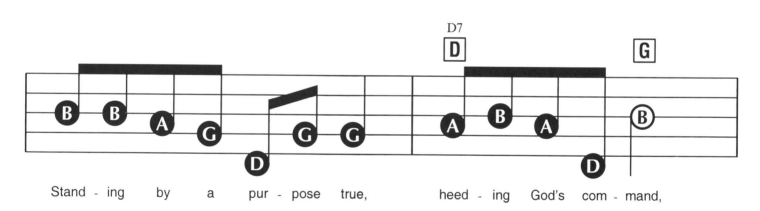

Stand - ing by a pur - pose true, heed - ing God's com - mand,

D.C. al Fine
(Return to beginning
Play to Fine)

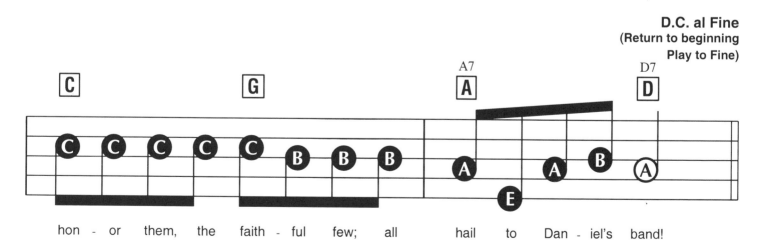

hon - or them, the faith - ful few; all hail to Dan - iel's band!

Deep and Wide

Registration 4
Rhythm: 8 Beat or Country

Traditional

Deep and wide, deep and wide, there's a
foun - tain flow - ing deep and wide.
Deep and wide, deep and wide, there's a
foun - tain flow - ing deep and wide. wide.

Dry Bones

Registration 3
Rhythm: Folk or Fox Trot

Traditional

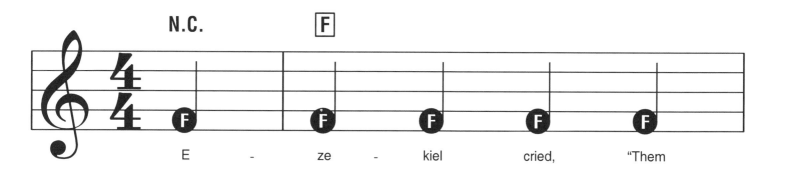

E - ze - kiel cried, "Them

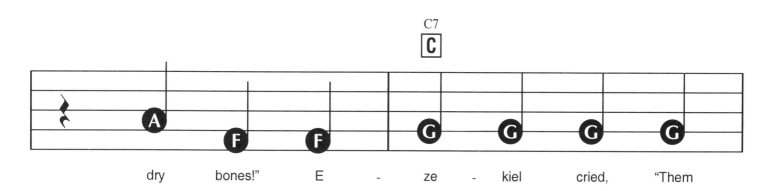

dry bones!" E - ze - kiel cried, "Them

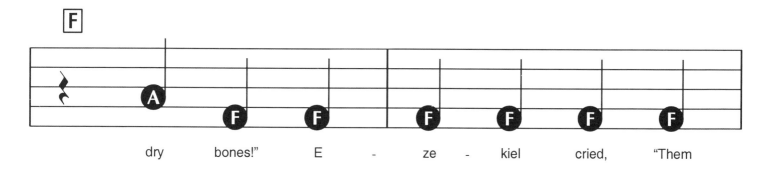

dry bones!" E - ze - kiel cried, "Them

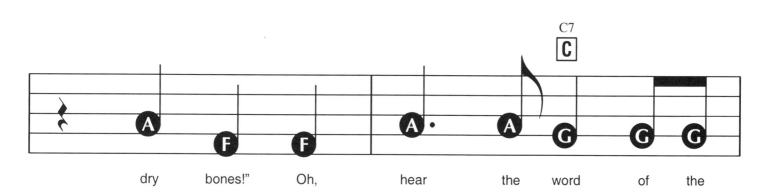

dry bones!" Oh, hear the word of the

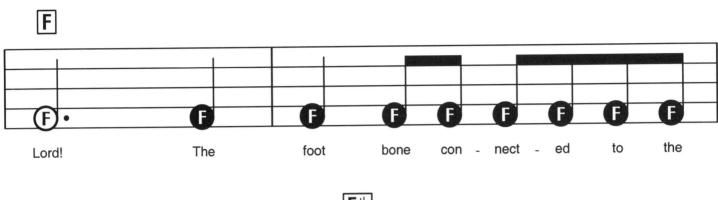

Lord! The foot bone con - nect - ed to the

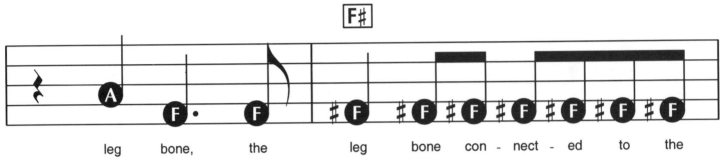

leg bone, the leg bone con - nect - ed to the

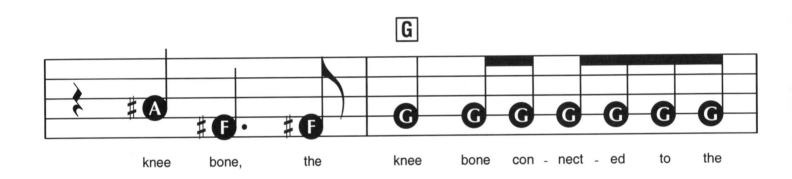

knee bone, the knee bone con - nect - ed to the

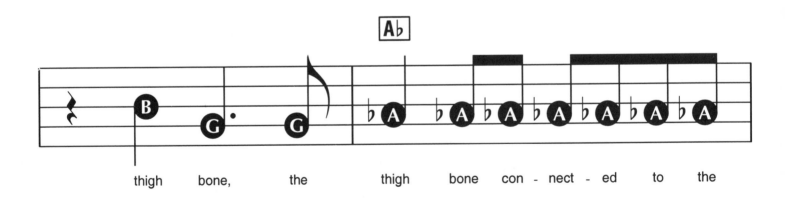

thigh bone, the thigh bone con - nect - ed to the

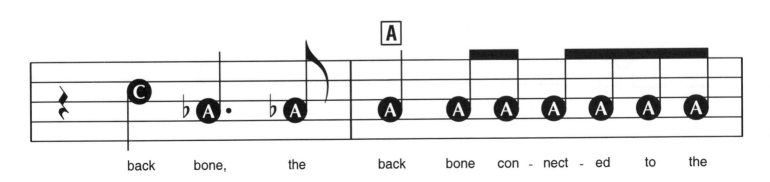

back bone, the back bone con - nect - ed to the

19

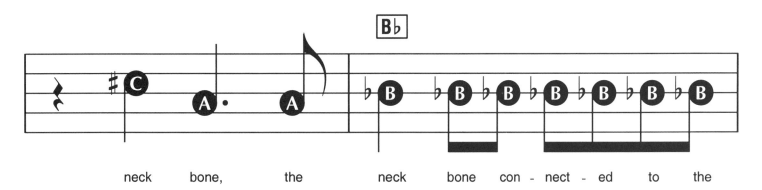

neck   bone,   the   neck   bone con - nect - ed   to   the

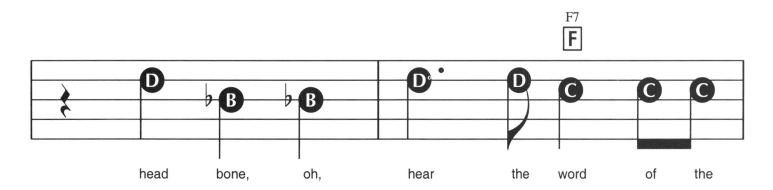

head   bone,   oh,   hear   the   word   of   the

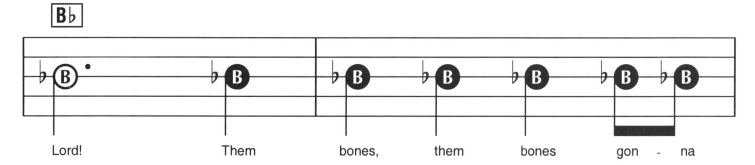

Lord!   Them   bones,   them   bones   gon - na

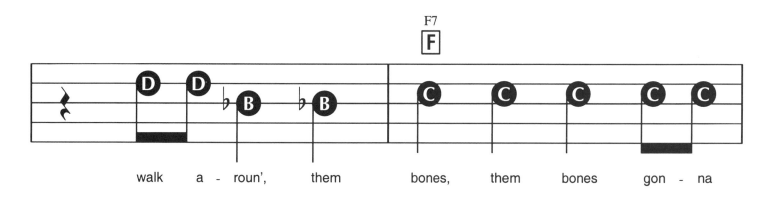

walk   a - roun',   them   bones,   them   bones   gon - na

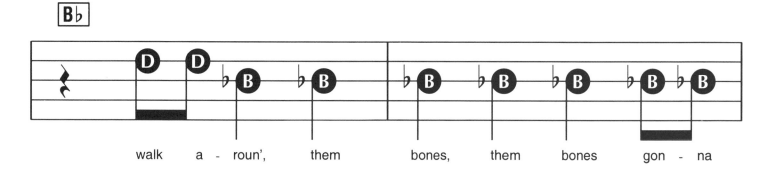

walk   a - roun',   them   bones,   them   bones   gon - na

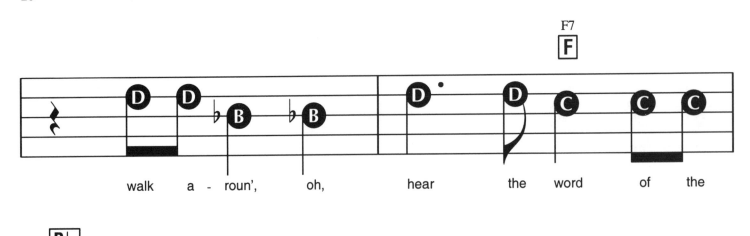

walk a - roun', oh, hear the word of the

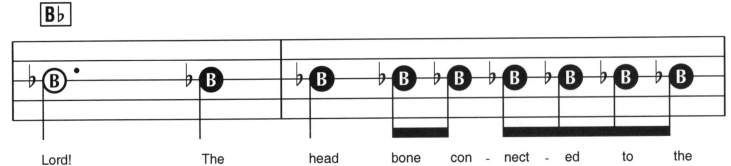

Lord! The head bone con - nect - ed to the

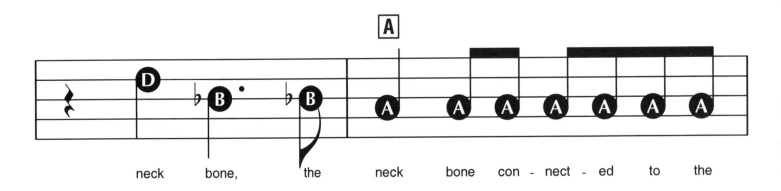

neck bone, the neck bone con - nect - ed to the

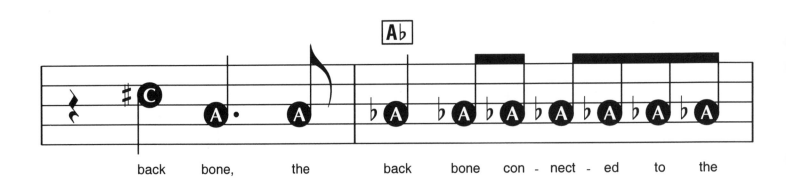

back bone, the back bone con - nect - ed to the

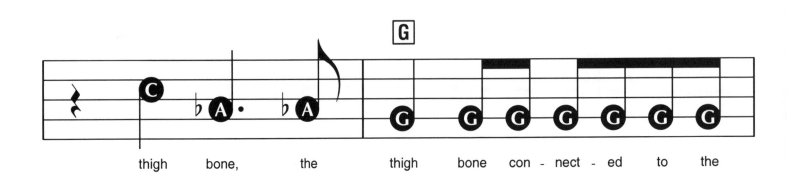

thigh bone, the thigh bone con - nect - ed to the

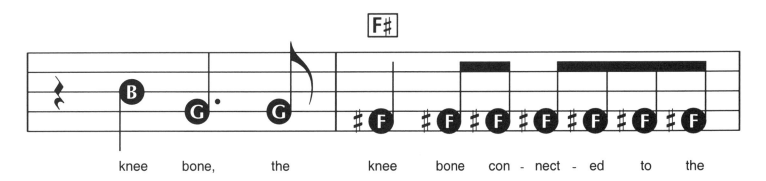

knee   bone,   the   knee   bone   con - nect - ed   to   the

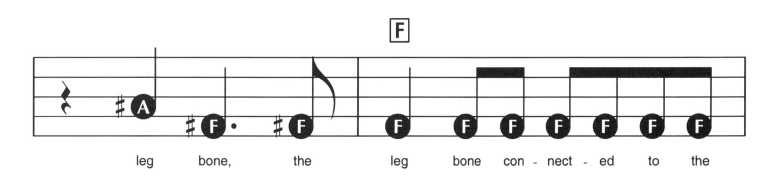

leg   bone,   the   leg   bone   con - nect - ed   to   the

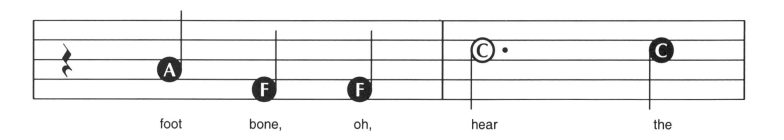

foot   bone,   oh,   hear   the

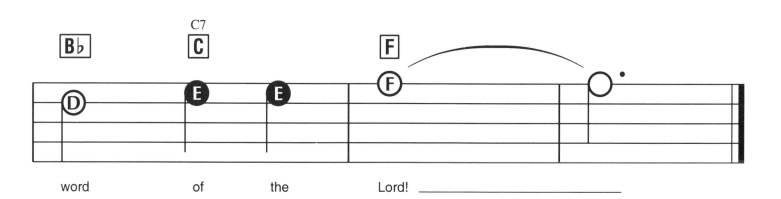

word   of   the   Lord! _____

21

Do Lord

Registration 3
Rhythm: Fox Trot

Traditional

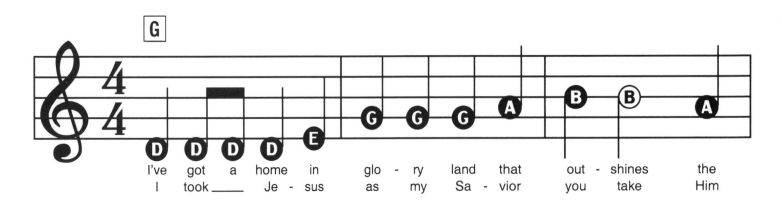

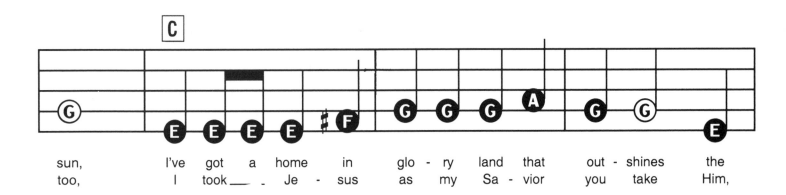

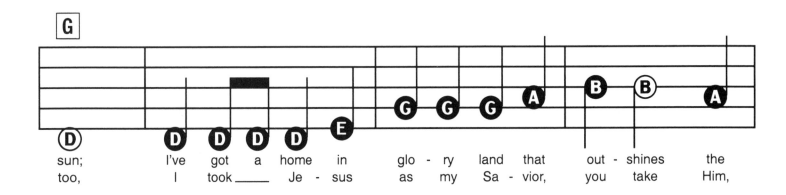

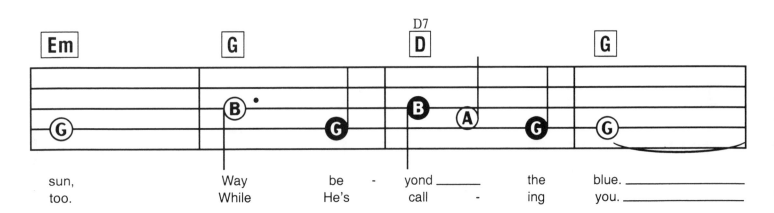

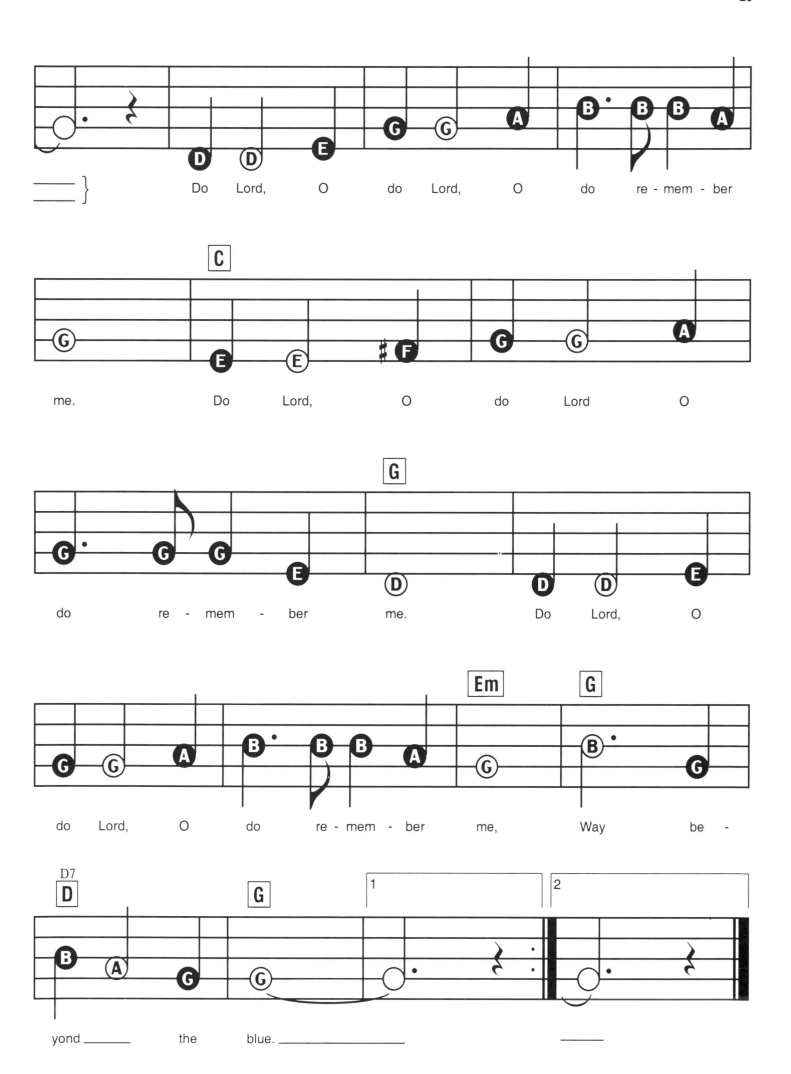

Down in My Heart

Registration 3
Rhythm: Fox Trot

Traditional

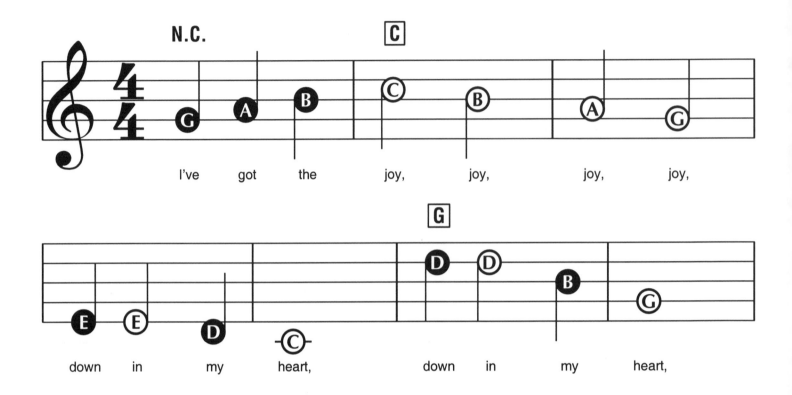

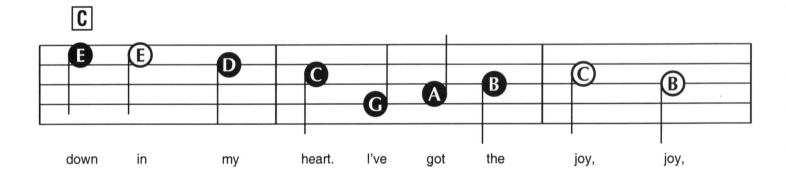

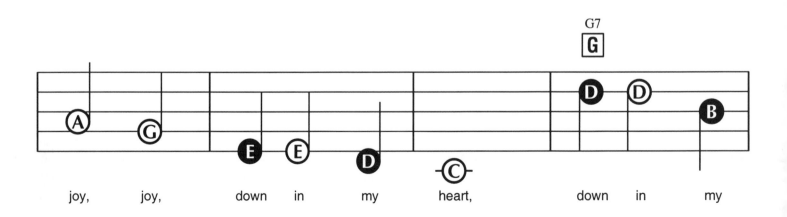

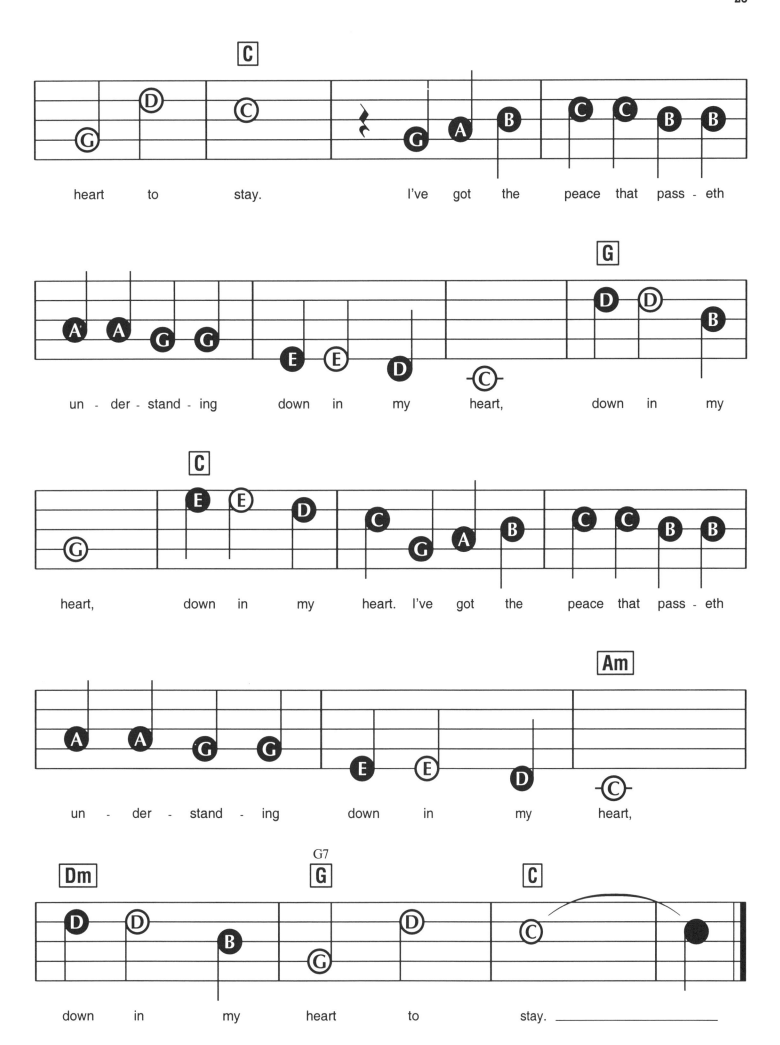

Every Time I Feel the Spirit

Registration 7
Rhythm: Rock or 8 Beat

African-American Spiritual

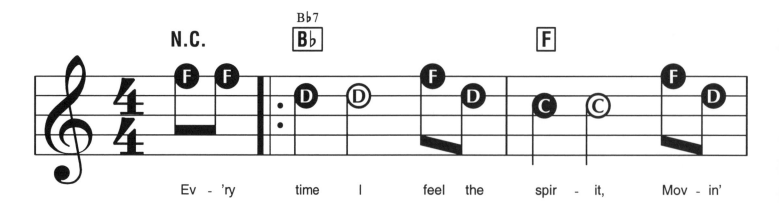

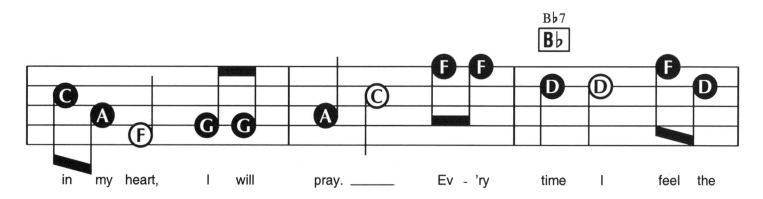

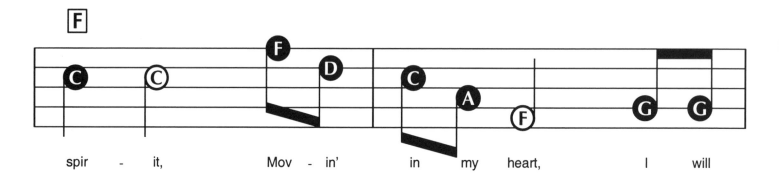

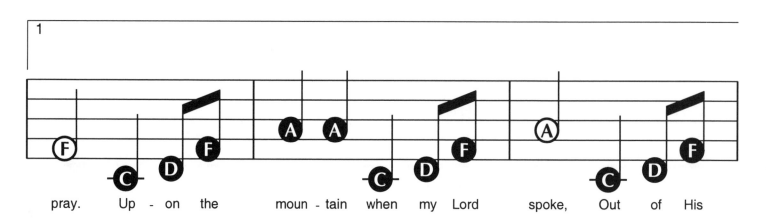

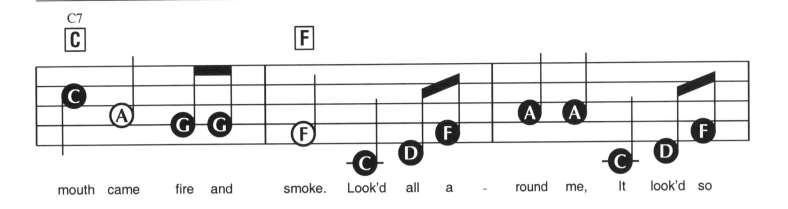

mouth came fire and smoke. Look'd all a - round me, It look'd so

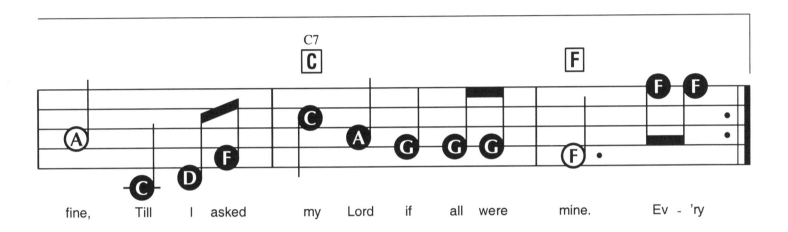

fine, Till I asked my Lord if all were mine. Ev - 'ry

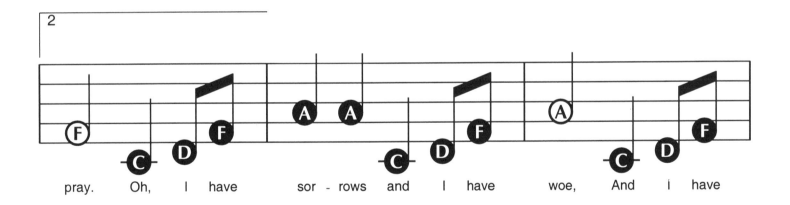

pray. Oh, I have sor - rows and I have woe, And i have

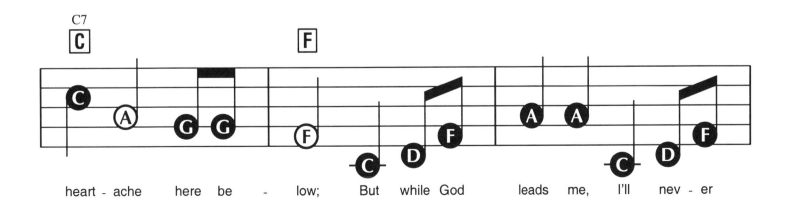

heart - ache here be - low; But while God leads me, I'll nev - er

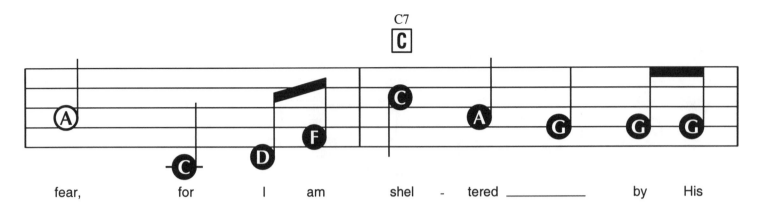

fear,   for   I   am   shel - tered _____ by   His

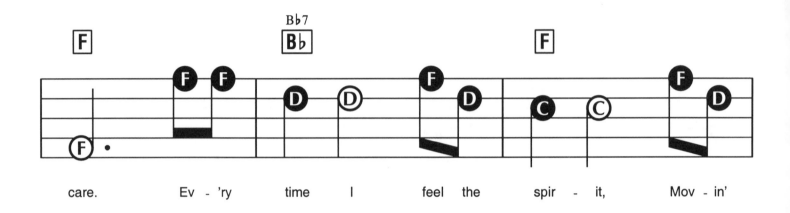

care.   Ev - 'ry   time   I   feel   the   spir - it,   Mov - in'

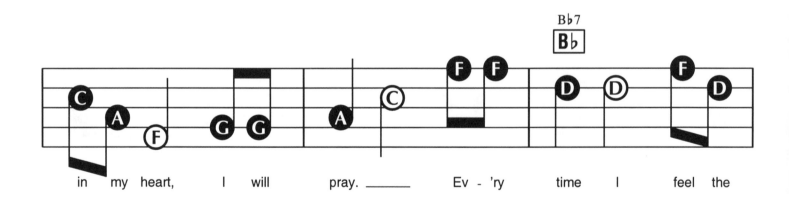

in   my   heart,   I   will   pray. _____ Ev - 'ry   time   I   feel   the

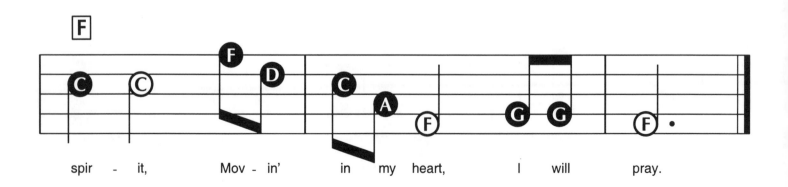

spir - it,   Mov - in'   in   my   heart,   I   will   pray.

Glory Be to God on High

Registration 4
Rhythm: Country or Ballad

Traditional

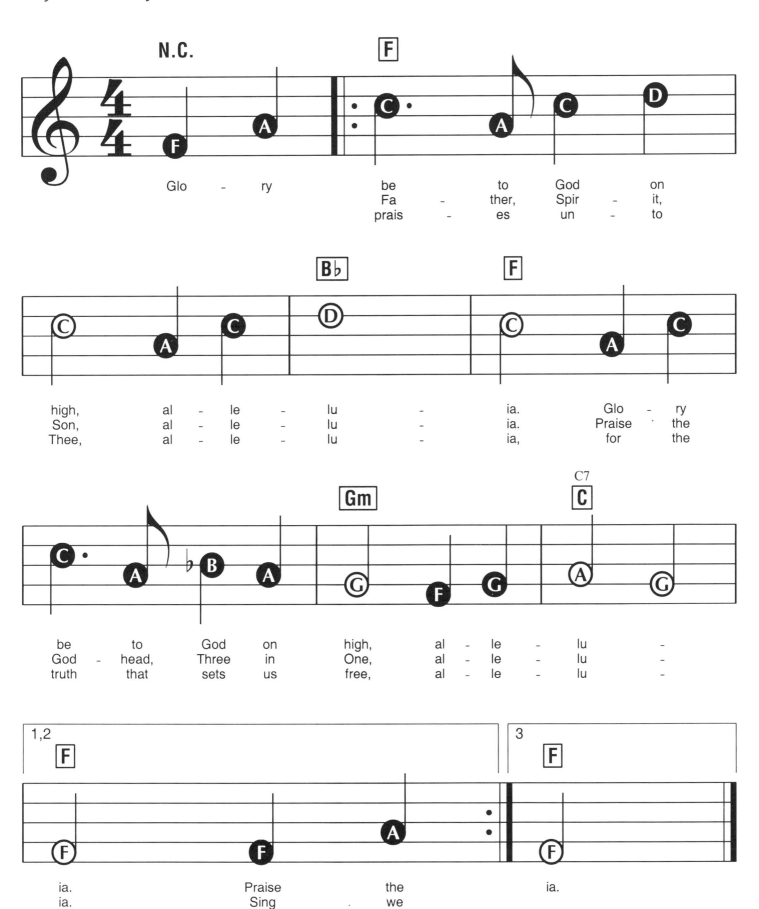

For the Beauty of the Earth

Registration 1
Rhythm: Ballad

Words by Folliot S. Pierpoint
Music by Conrad Kocher

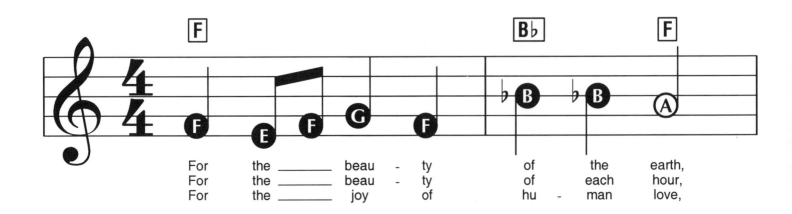

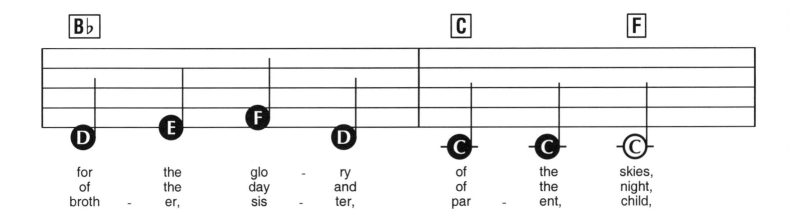

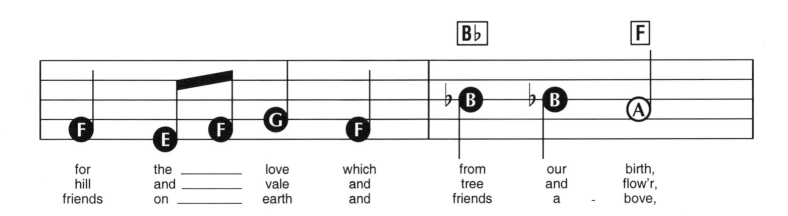

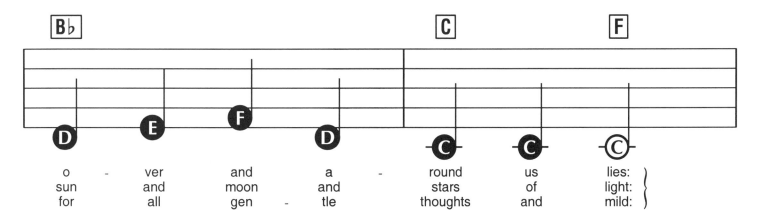

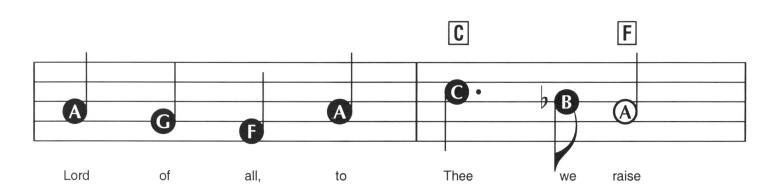

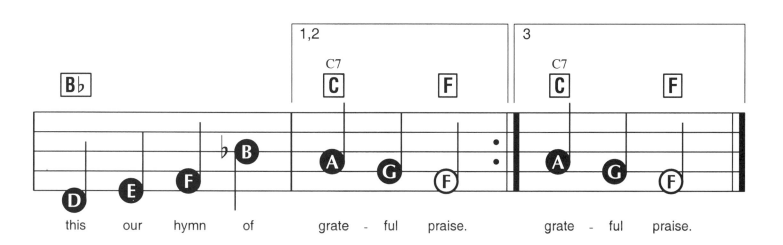

Give Me Oil in My Lamp

Registration 8
Rhythm: Country

Traditional

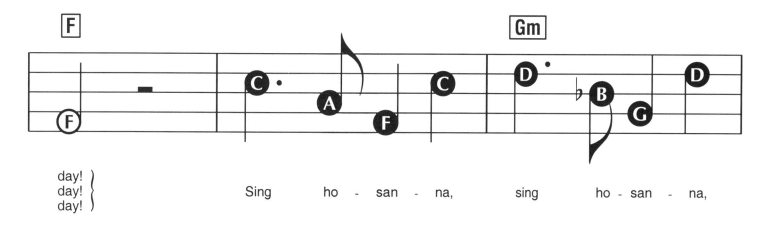

day!
day!
day!
Sing ho - san - na, sing ho - san - na,

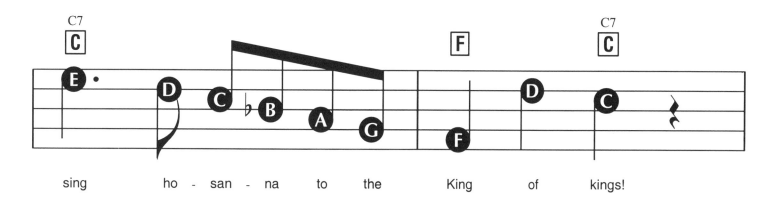

sing ho - san - na to the King of kings!

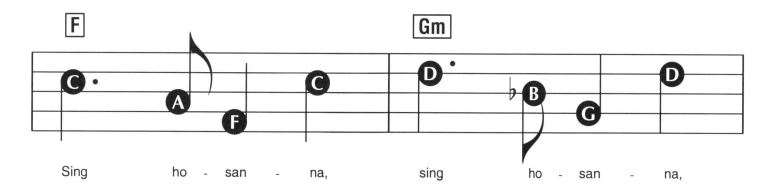

Sing ho - san - na, sing ho - san - na,

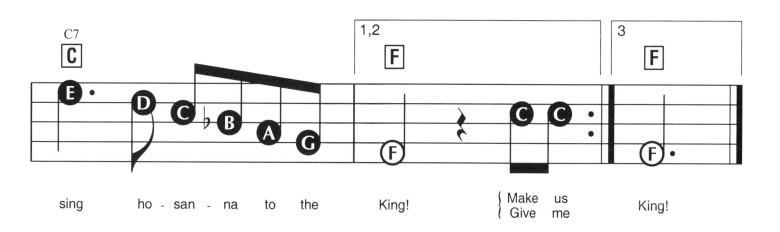

sing ho - san - na to the King!
Make us
Give me
King!

God Is So Good

Registration 8
Rhythm: Ballad or Country

Traditional

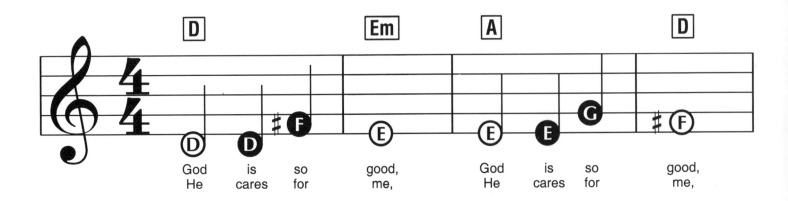

God is so good,
He cares so for me,
God is so good,
He cares so for me,

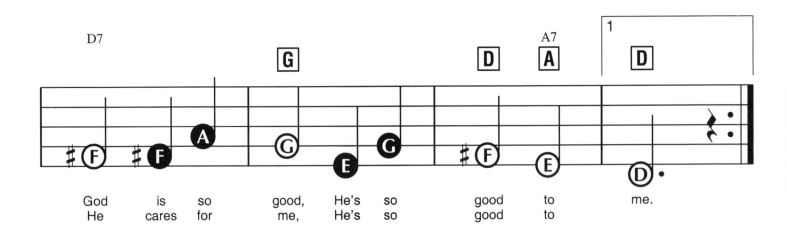

God is so good,
He cares so for me,
He's so good,
He's so good to me,
good to me.
good to

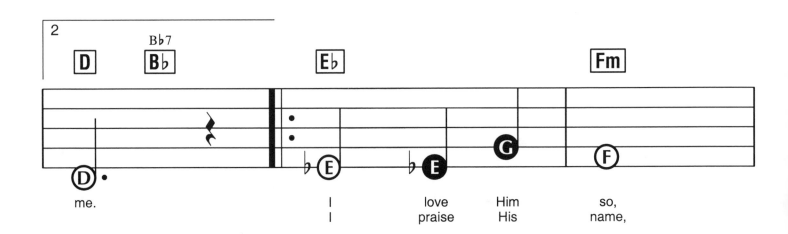

me.
I love Him so,
I praise His name,

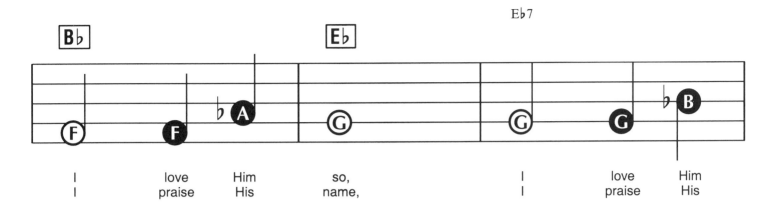

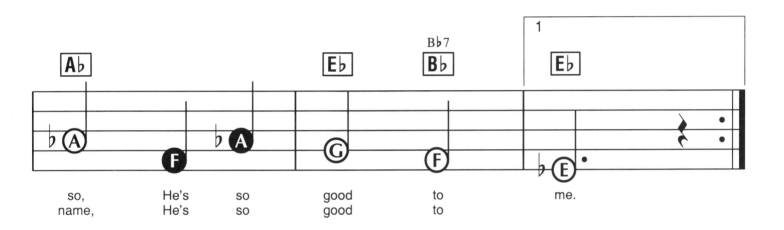

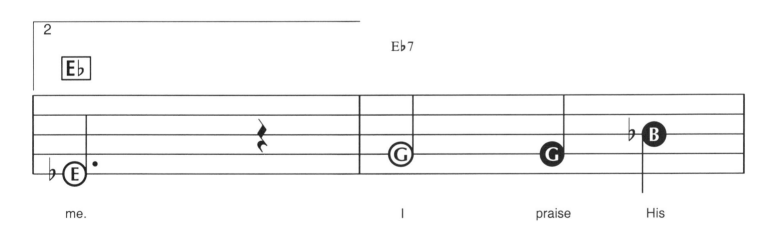

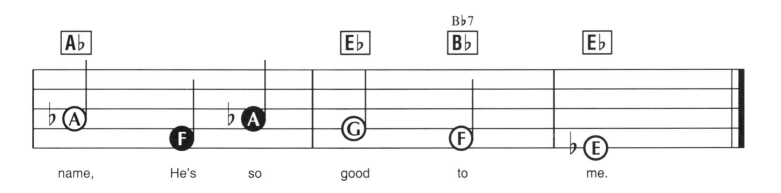

The Gospel Train

Registration 4
Rhythm: Gospel or Fox Trot

African-American Spiritual

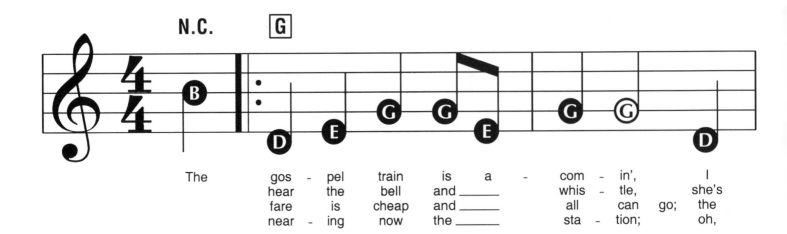

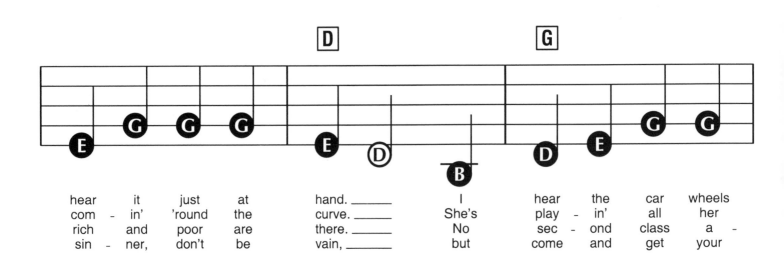

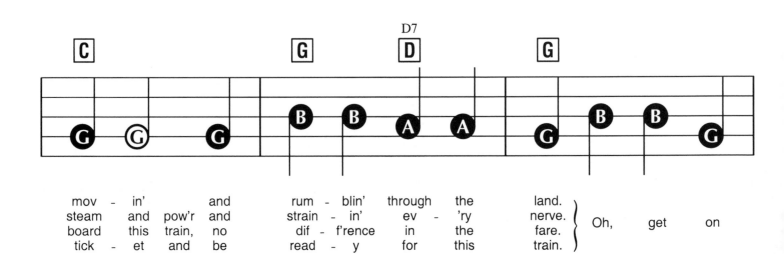

37

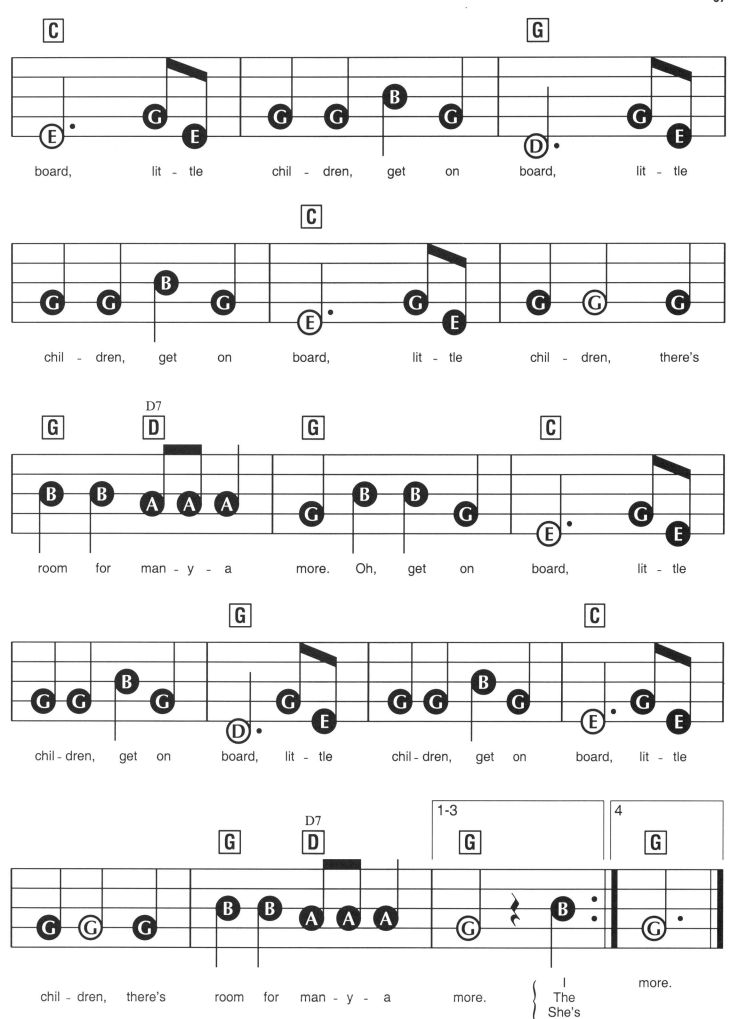

Great Day

Registration 2
Rhythm: March

Traditional Spiritual

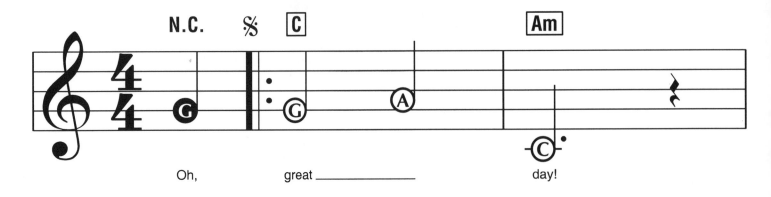

Oh, great _____ day!

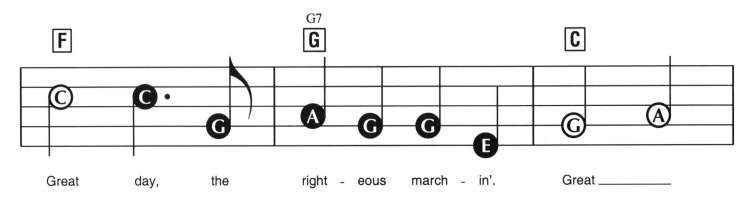

Great day, the right-eous march-in'. Great _____

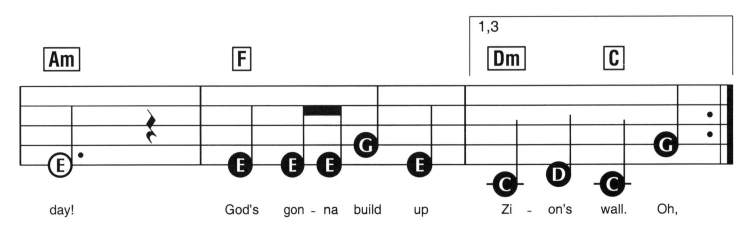

day! God's gon-na build up Zi-on's wall. Oh,

1,3

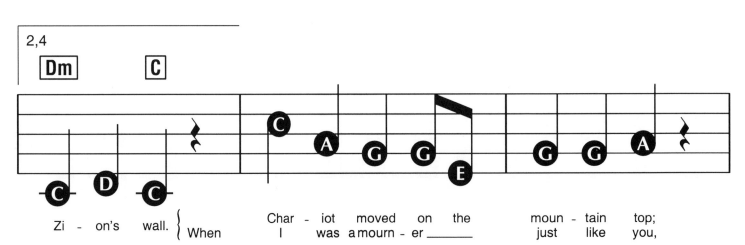

2,4

Zi-on's wall. { When Char-iot moved on the moun-tain top;
I was a mourn-er _____ just like you,

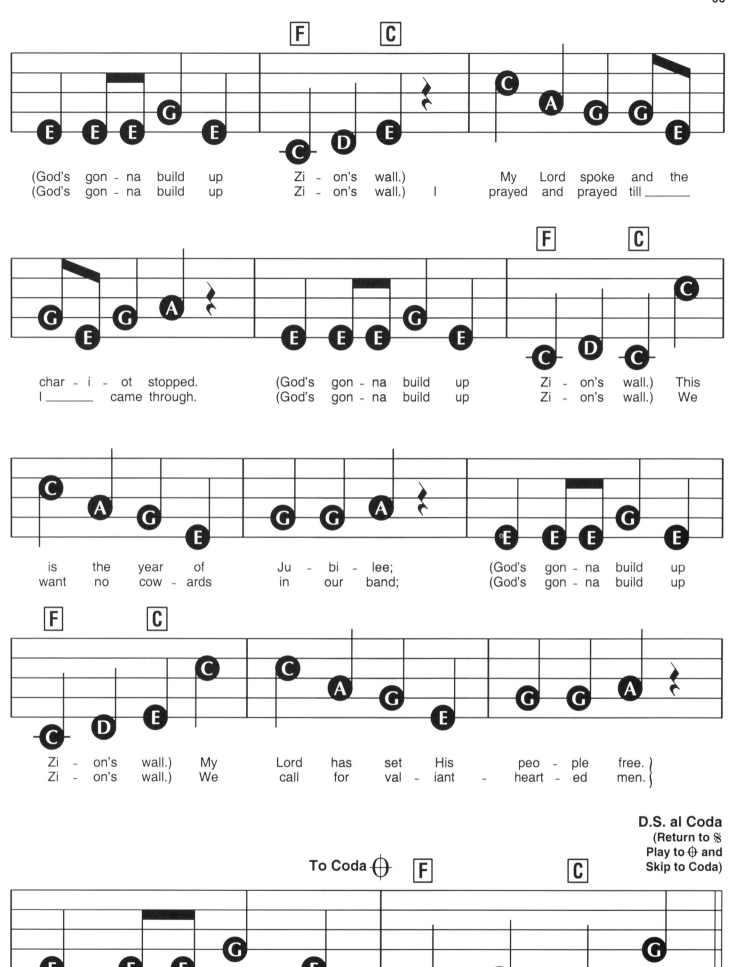

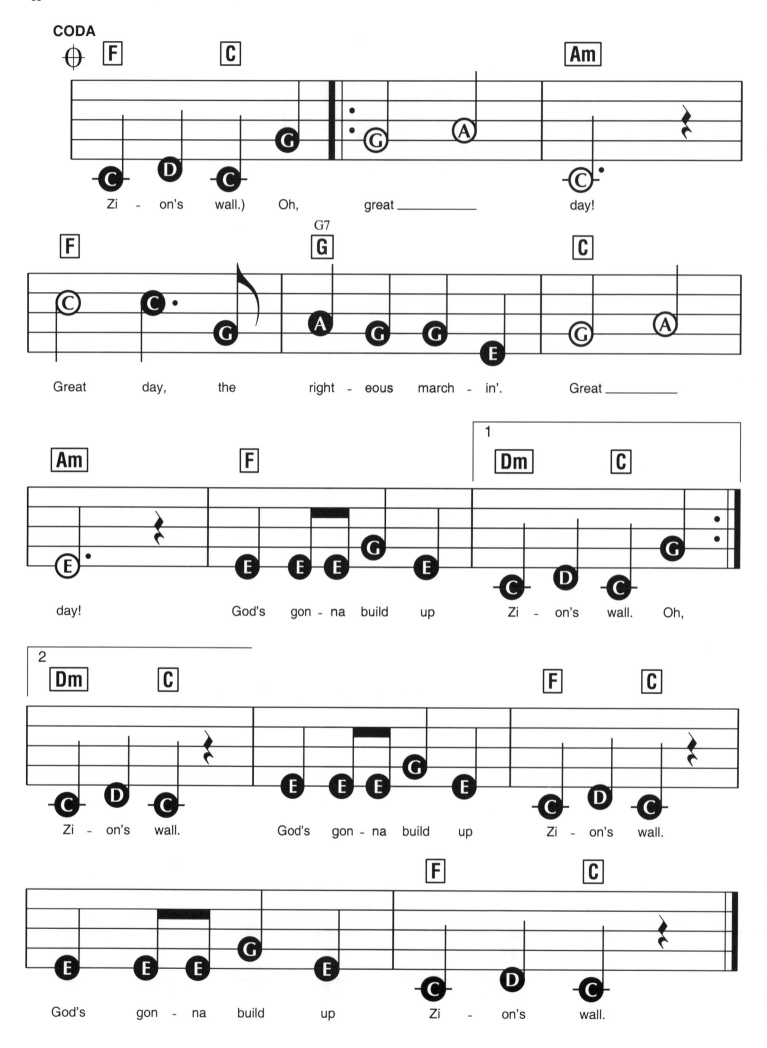

Ho-Ho-Ho-Hosanna

Registration 9
Rhythm: Fox Trot

Traditional

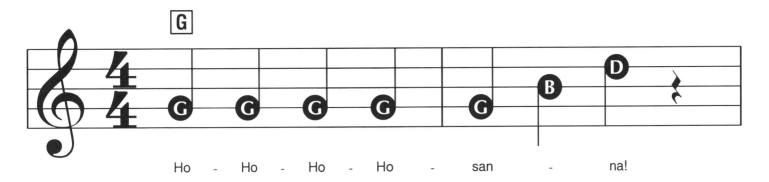

Ho - Ho - Ho - Ho - san - na!

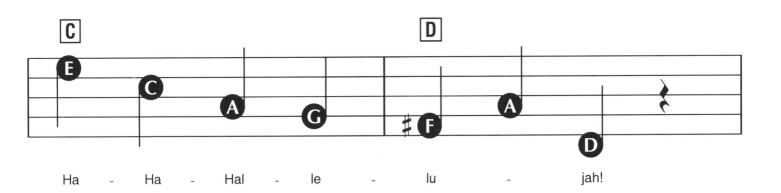

Ha - Ha - Hal - le - lu - jah!

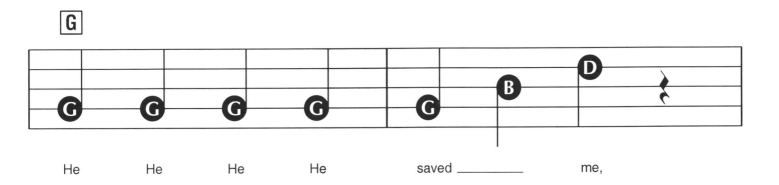

He   He   He   He   saved _____ me,

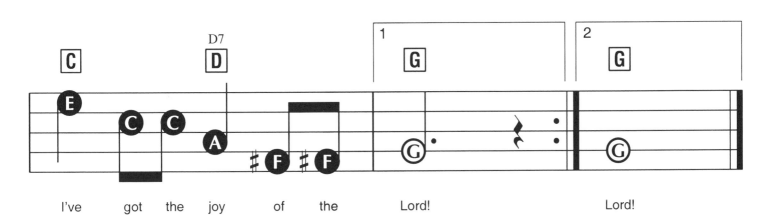

I've got the joy of the Lord!   Lord!

Hallelu, Hallelujah!

Registration 8
Rhythm: Country or Swing

Traditional

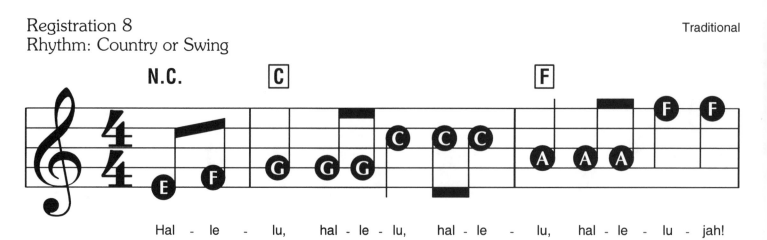

Hal - le - lu, hal - le - lu, hal - le - lu, hal - le - lu - jah!

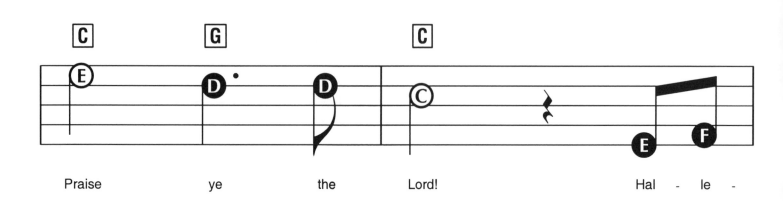

Praise   ye   the   Lord!   Hal - le -

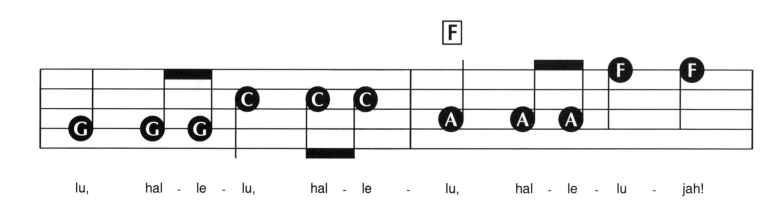

lu,   hal - le - lu,   hal - le - lu,   hal - le - lu - jah!

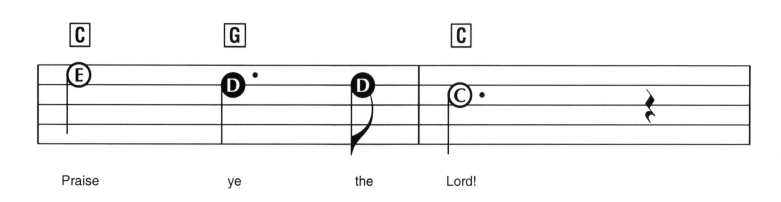

Praise   ye   the   Lord!

43

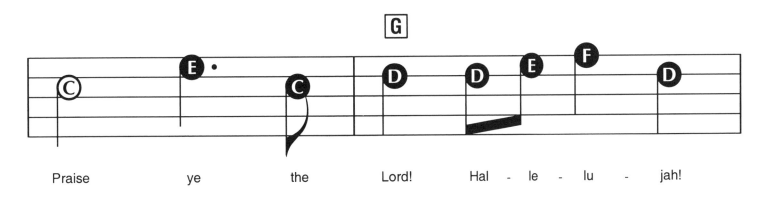

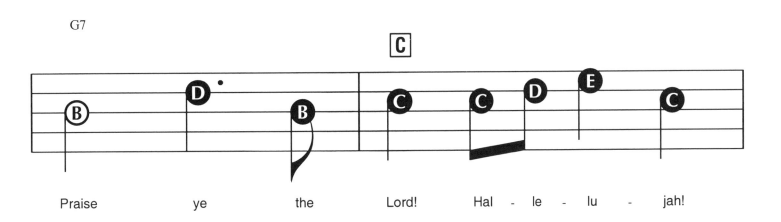

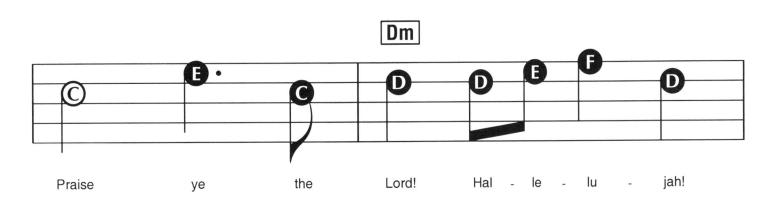

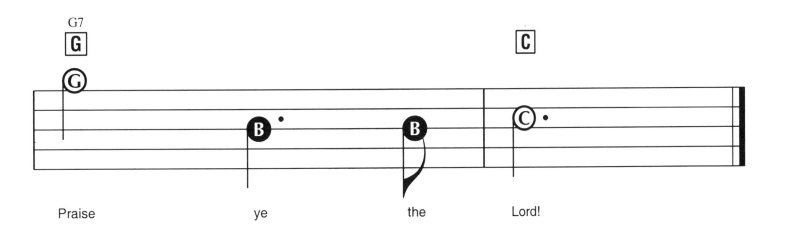

He's Got the Whole World in His Hands

Registration 6
Rhythm: Fox Trot or Swing

Traditional Spiritual

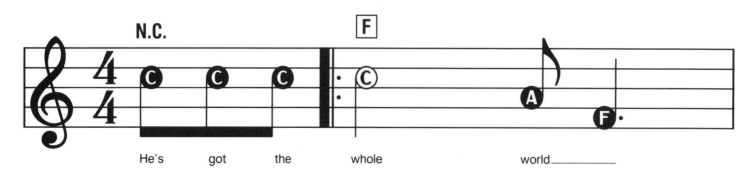

He's got the whole world____

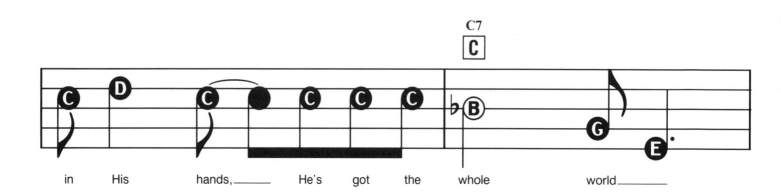

in His hands,____ He's got the whole world____

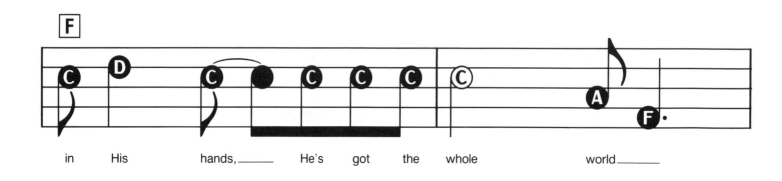

in His hands,____ He's got the whole world____

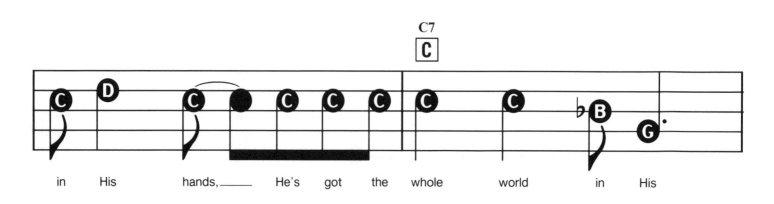

in His hands,____ He's got the whole world in His

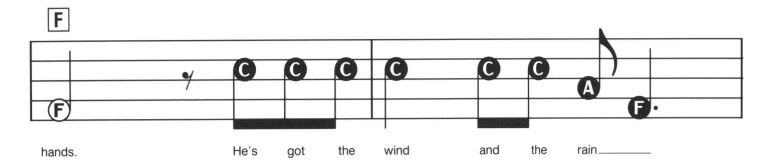

hands. He's got the wind and the rain

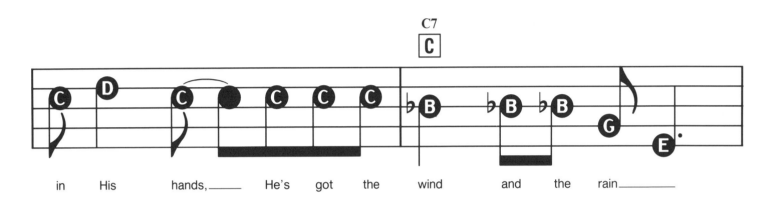

in His hands,____ He's got the wind and the rain____

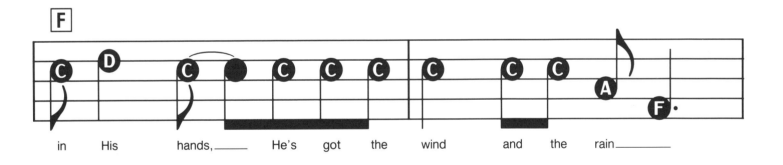

in His hands,____ He's got the wind and the rain____

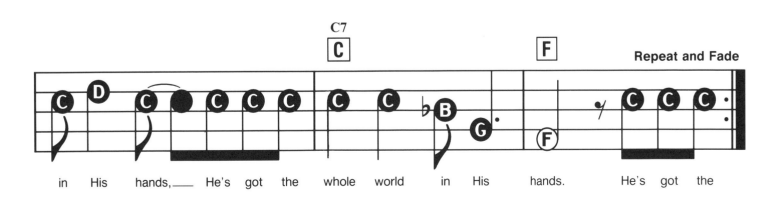

in His hands,____ He's got the whole world in His hands. He's got the

His Banner Over Me Is Love

Registration 8
Rhythm: Country or 8 Beat

Text based on Song Of Solomon 2:4, 16
Traditional Music

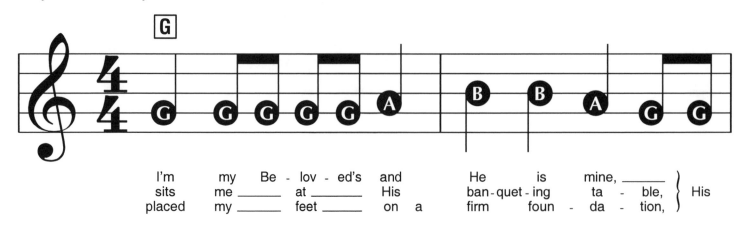

I'm   my   Be - lov - ed's   and   He   is   mine, _____   His
sits   me _____ at _____ His   ban - quet - ing   ta - ble,
placed   my _____ feet _____ on   a   firm   foun - da - tion,

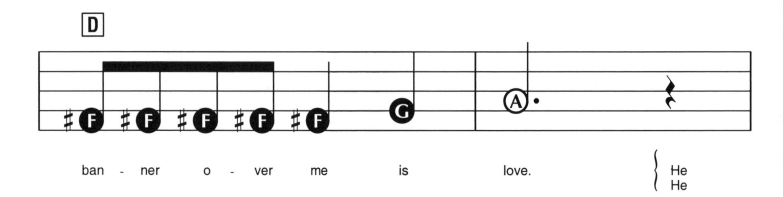

ban - ner   o - ver   me   is   love.   He
                                           He

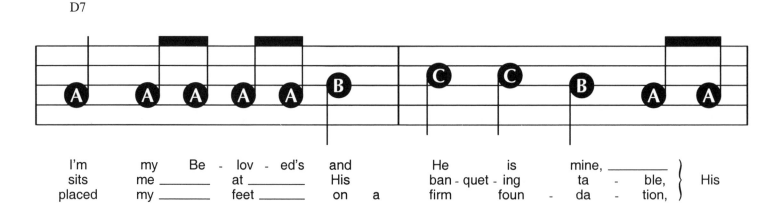

I'm   my   Be - lov - ed's   and   He   is   mine, _____   His
sits   me _____ at _____ His   ban - quet - ing   ta - ble,
placed   my _____ feet _____ on   a   firm   foun - da - tion,

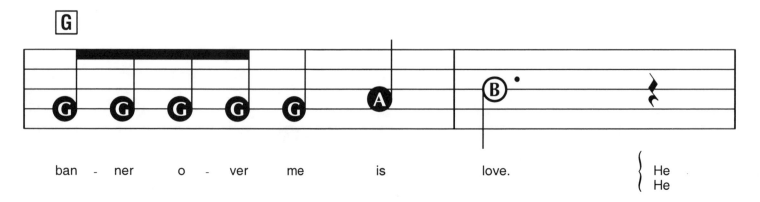

ban - ner   o - ver   me   is   love.   He
                                           He

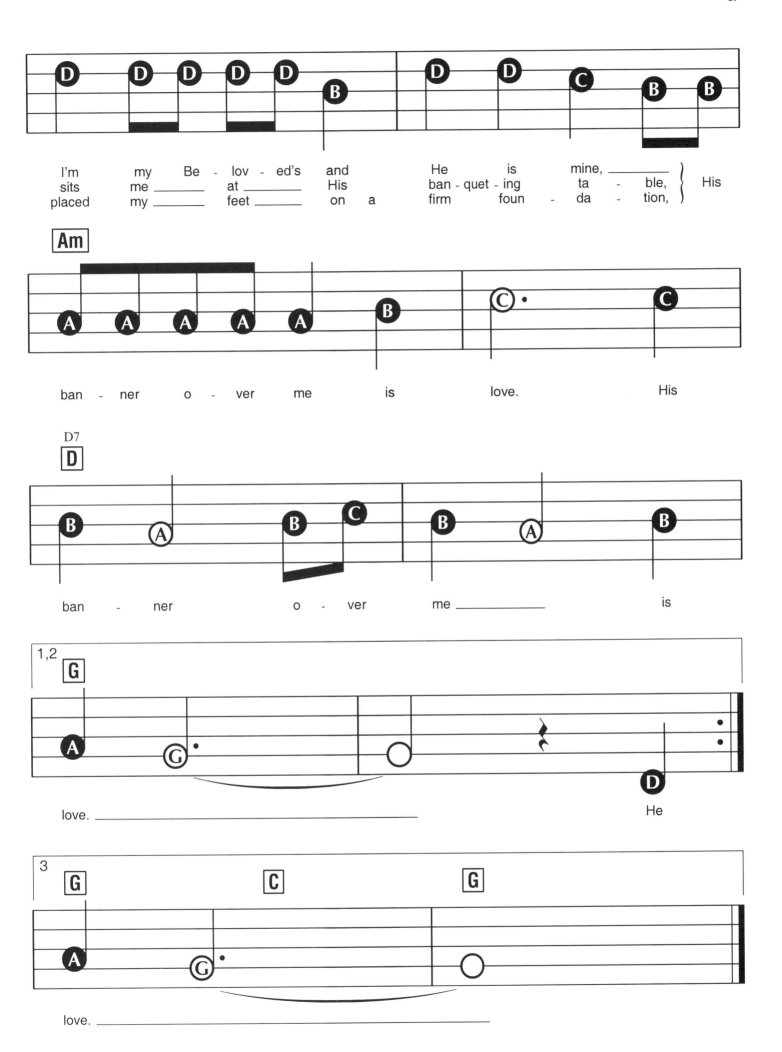

I Am a C-H-R-I-S-T-I-A-N

Registration 5
Rhythm: March or Fox Trot

Traditional

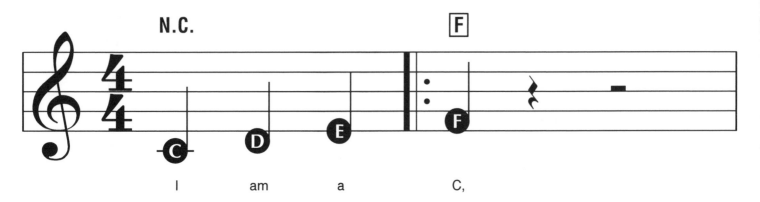

I am a C,

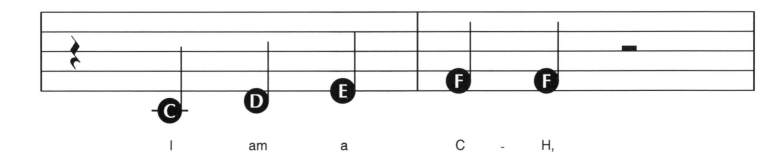

I am a C - H,

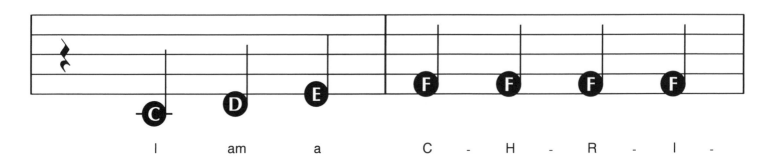

I am a C - H - R - I -

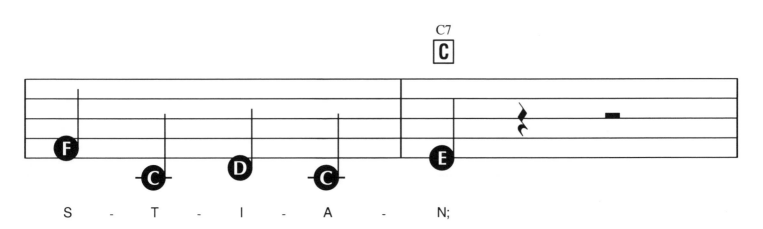

S - T - I - A - N;

49

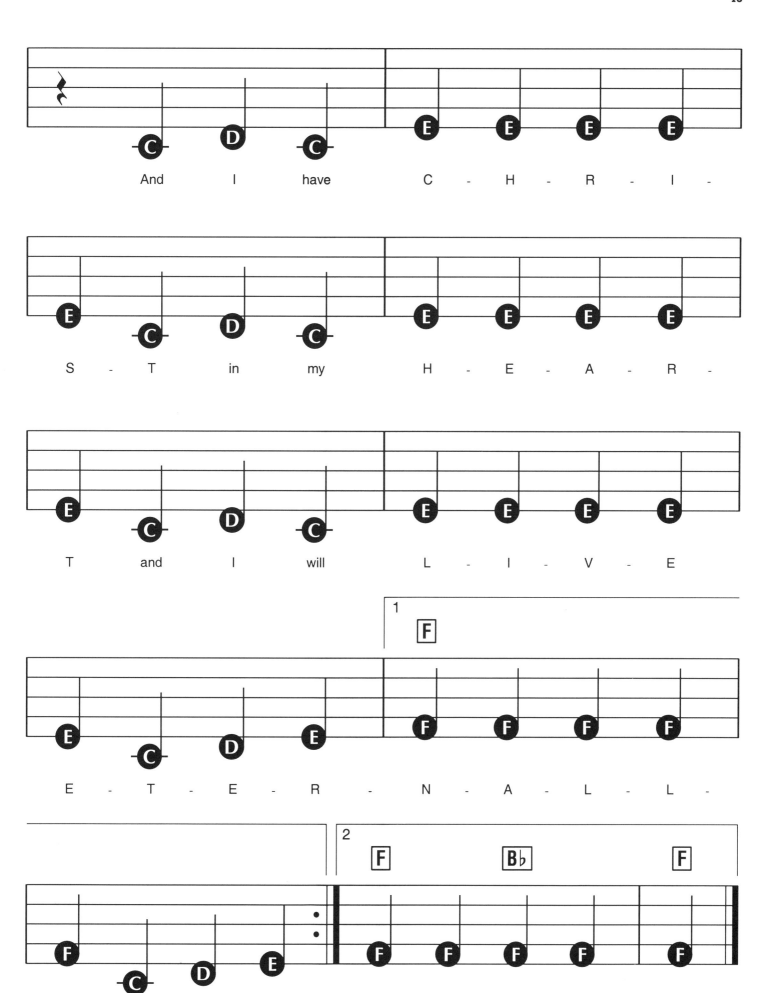

I Will Sing of the Mercies

Registration 7
Rhythm: March or Gospel

Words based on Psalm 89:1
Music by James H. Fillmore

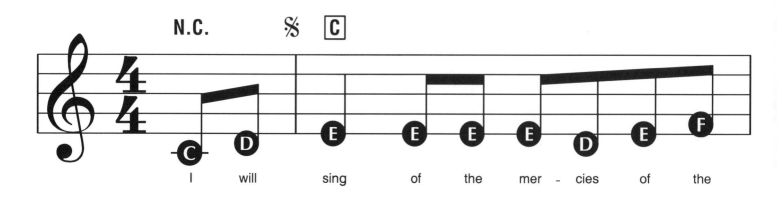

I will sing of the mer - cies of the

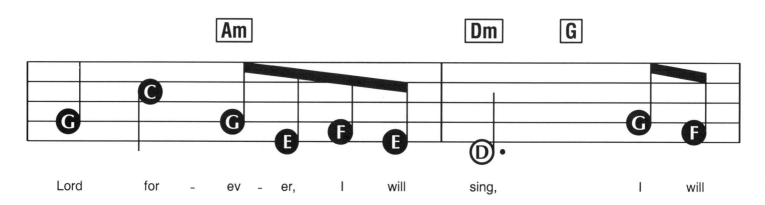

Lord for - ev - er, I will sing, I will

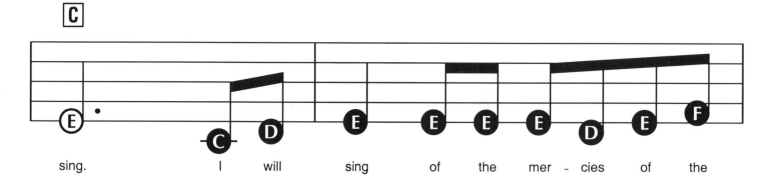

sing. I will sing of the mer - cies of the

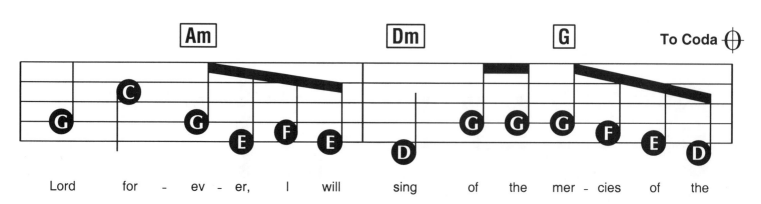

Lord for - ev - er, I will sing of the mer - cies of the

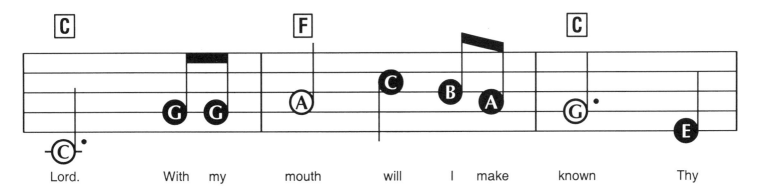

Lord. With my mouth will I make known Thy

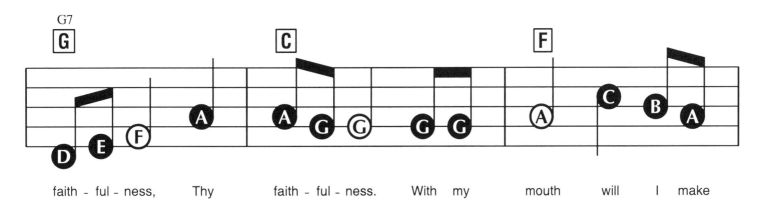

faith - ful - ness, Thy faith - ful - ness. With my mouth will I make

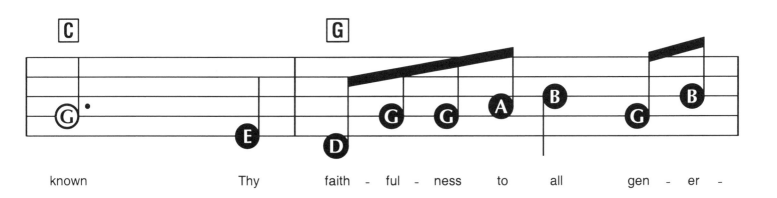

known Thy faith - ful - ness to all gen - er -

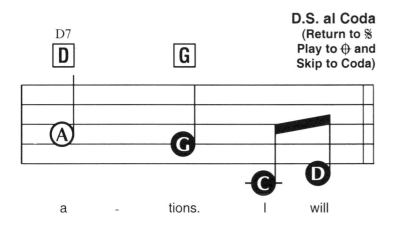

D.S. al Coda
(Return to 𝄋
Play to ⊕ and
Skip to Coda)

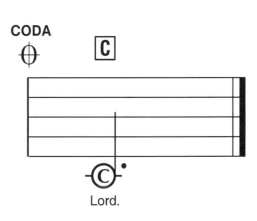

a - tions. I will

CODA

Lord.

I'll Be a Sunbeam

Registration 10
Rhythm: Waltz

Words by Nellie Talbot
Music by Edwin O. Excell

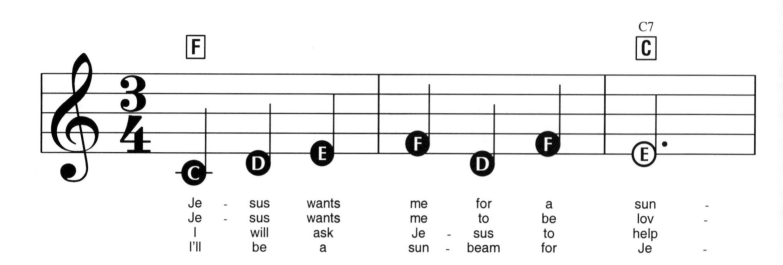

Je - sus wants me for a sun -
Je - sus wants me to be lov -
I will ask Je - sus to help
I'll be a sun - beam for Je -

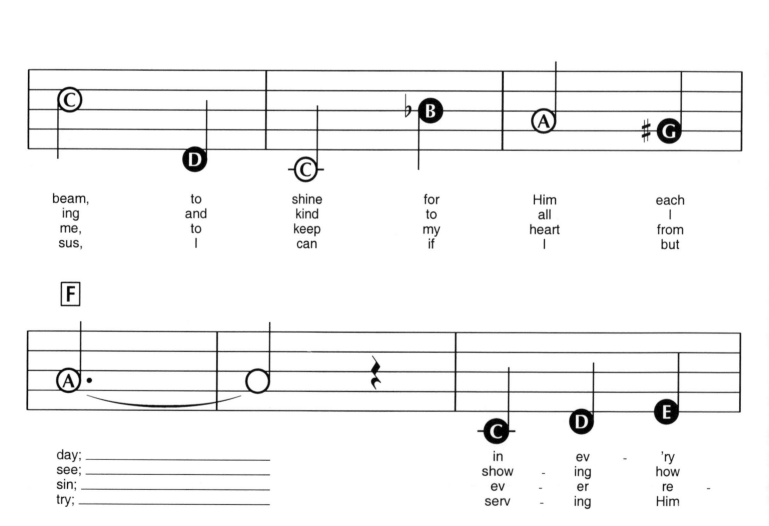

beam, to shine for Him each
ing, and kind to all I
me, I keep my if I from
sus, I can if heart but

day; _____
see; _____
sin; _____
try; _____

in ev - 'ry
show - ing how
ev - er re -
serv - ing Him

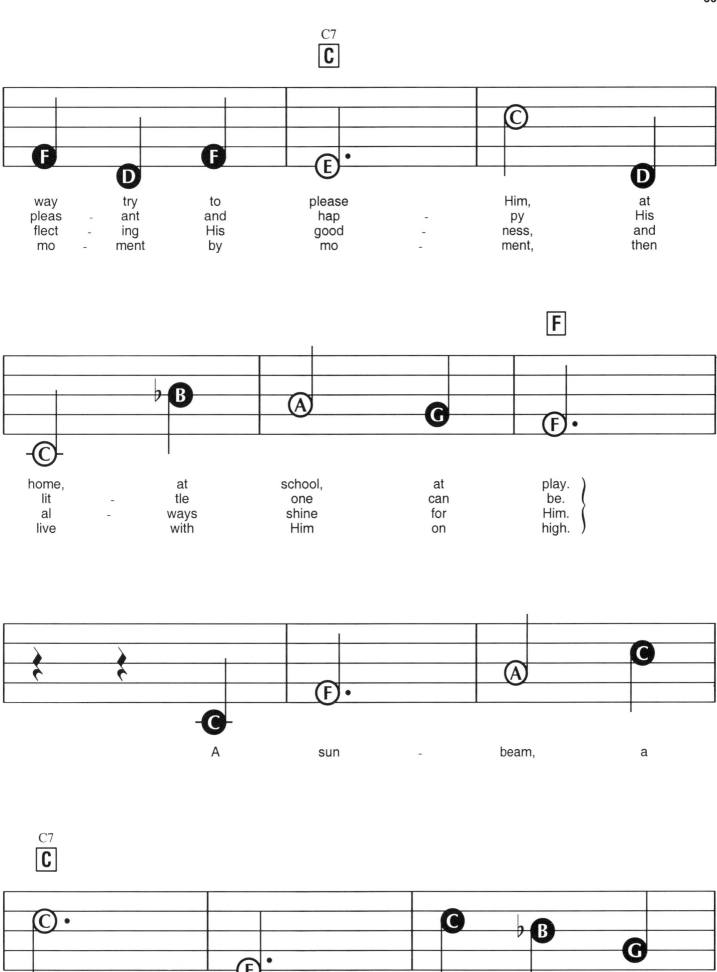

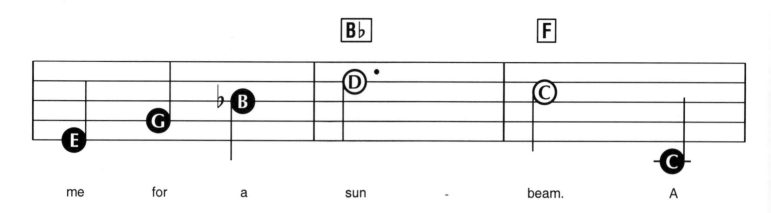

me   for   a   sun   -   beam.   A

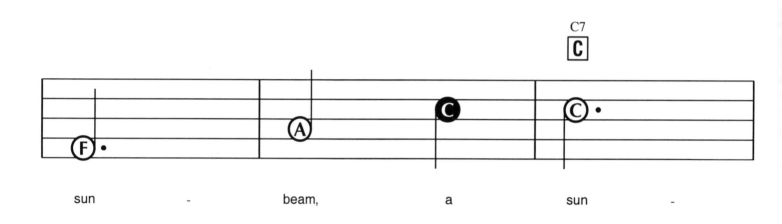

sun   -   beam,   a   sun   -

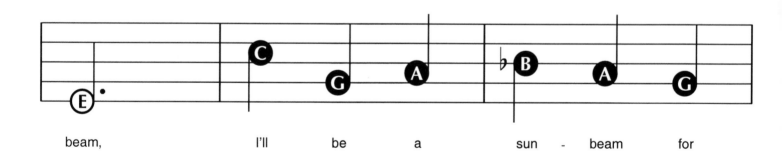

beam,   I'll   be   a   sun - beam   for

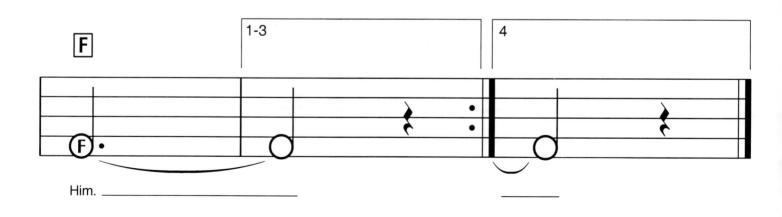

Him. _____

Jesus Bids Us Shine

Registration 4
Rhythm: Country or Fox Trot

Words by Susan Warner
Music by Edwin Excell

I'm Gonna Sing, Sing, Sing

Registration 8
Rhythm: Fox Trot

Traditional

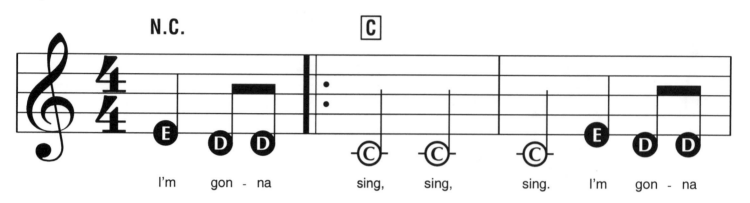

I'm   gon - na   sing,   sing,   sing.   I'm   gon - na

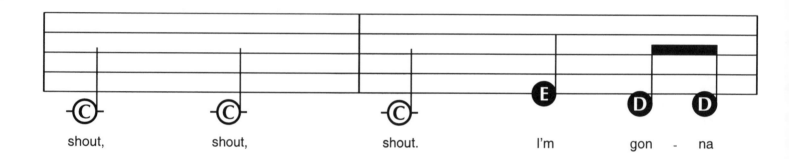

shout,   shout,   shout.   I'm   gon - na

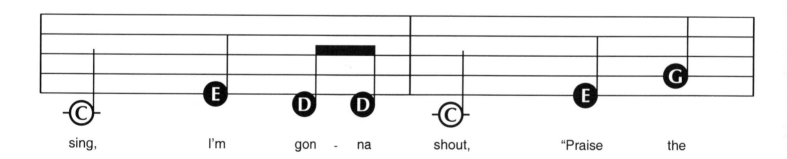

sing,   I'm   gon - na   shout,   "Praise   the

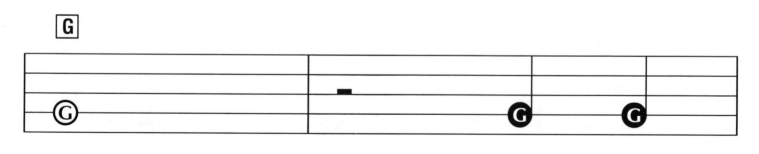

Lord!"   When   those

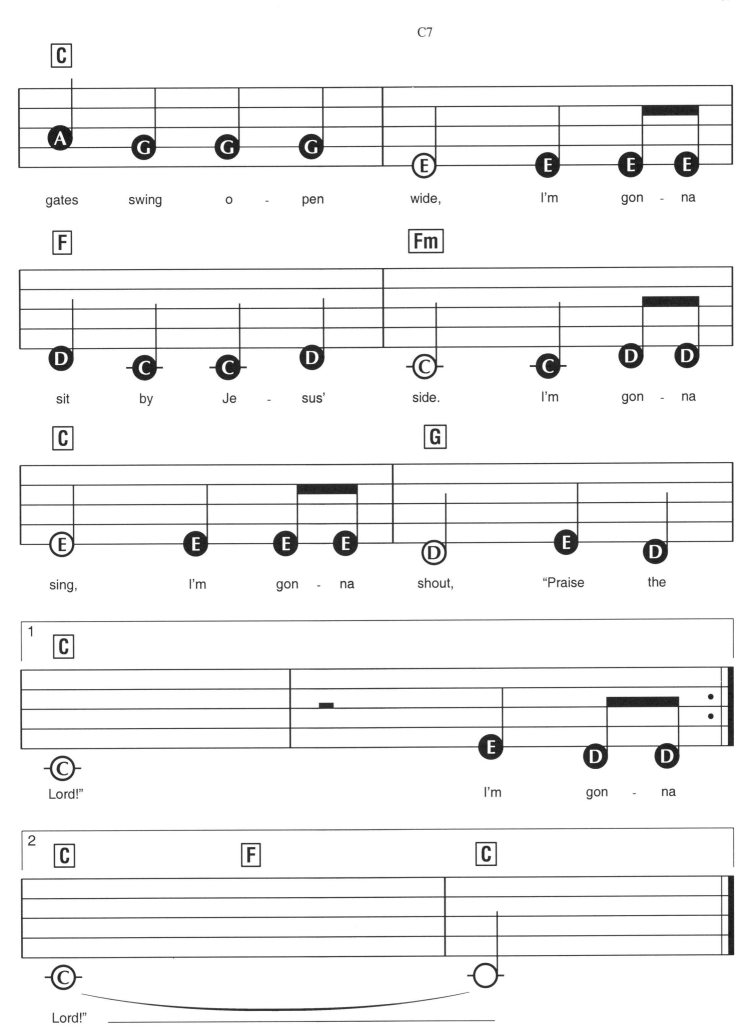

I'm Gonna Sing When the Spirit Says Sing

Registration 8
Rhythm: Gospel

African-American Spiritual

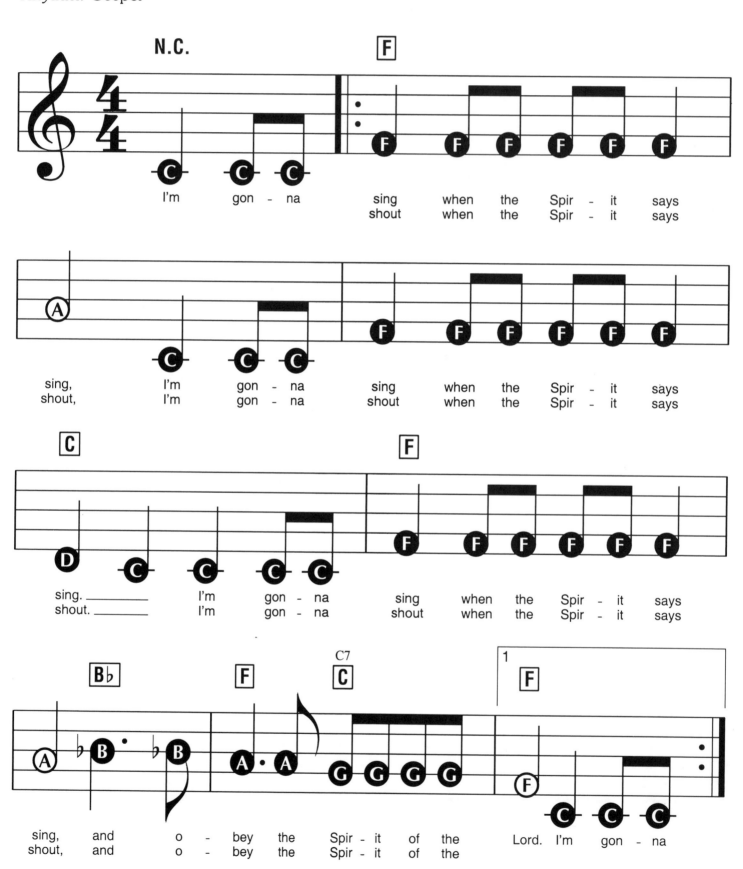

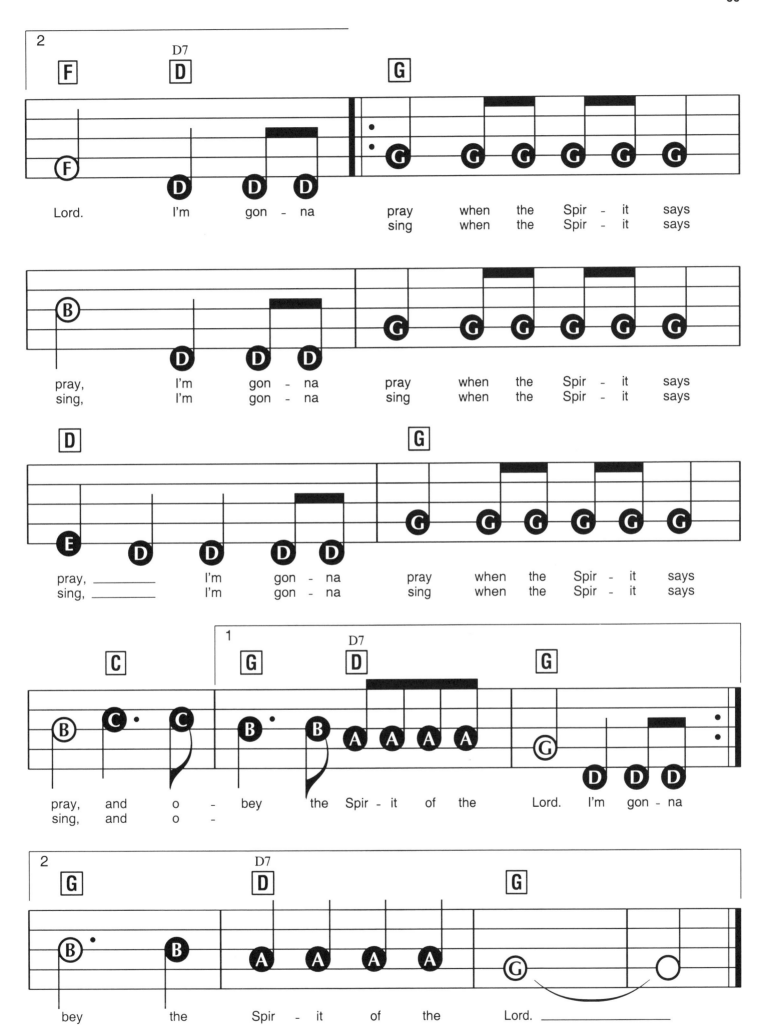

I'm in the Lord's Army

Registration 7
Rhythm: March

Traditional

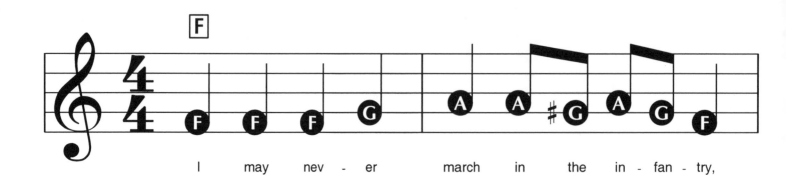

I may nev - er march in the in - fan - try,

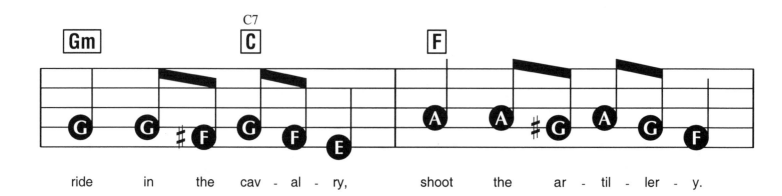

ride in the cav - al - ry, shoot the ar - til - ler - y.

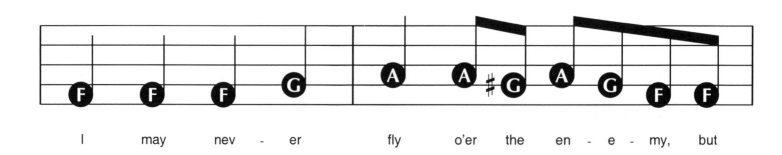

I may nev - er fly o'er the en - e - my, but

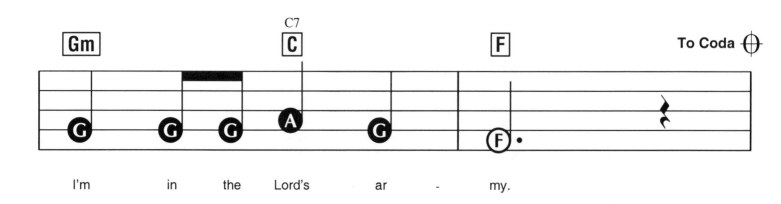

I'm in the Lord's ar - my.

61

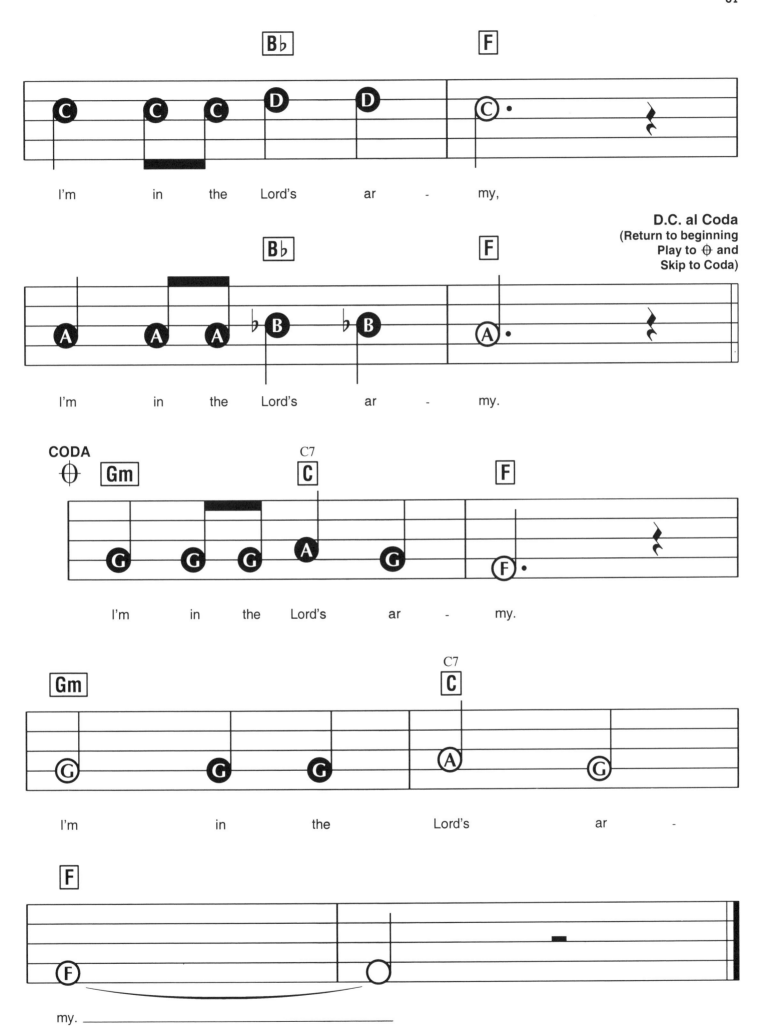

I've Got Peace Like a River

Registration 8
Rhythm: Ballad or Fox Trot

Traditional

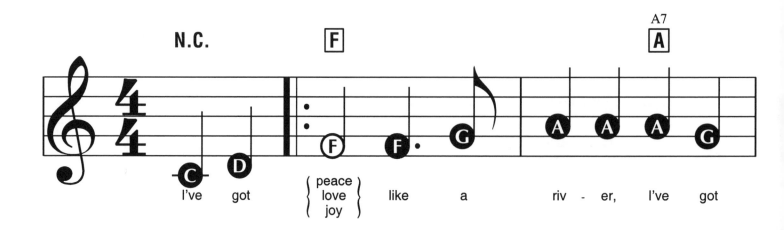

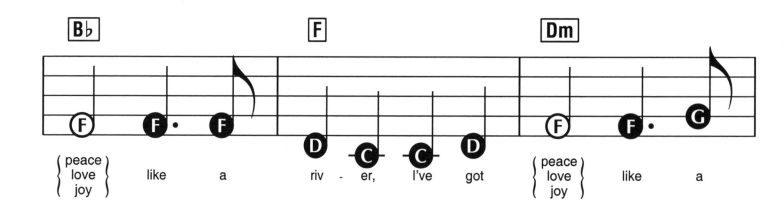

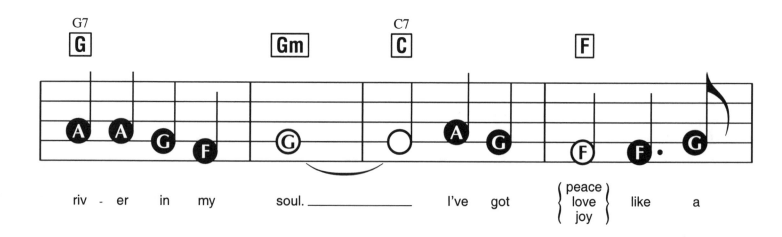

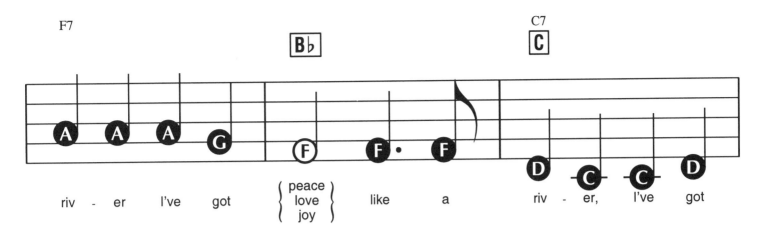

riv - er I've got { peace love joy } like a riv - er, I've got

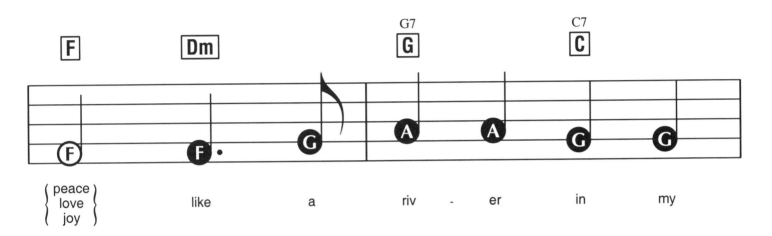

{ peace love joy } like a riv - er in my

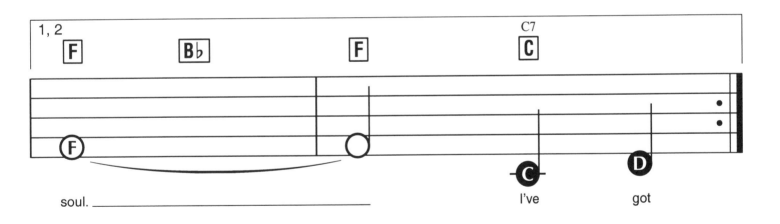

soul. _____ I've got

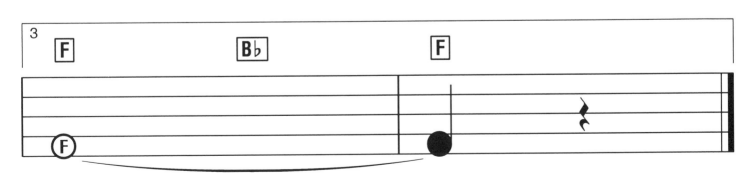

soul. _____

If You're Happy and You Know It

Registration 4
Rhythm: Waltz or 6/8 March

Words and Music by
L. Smith

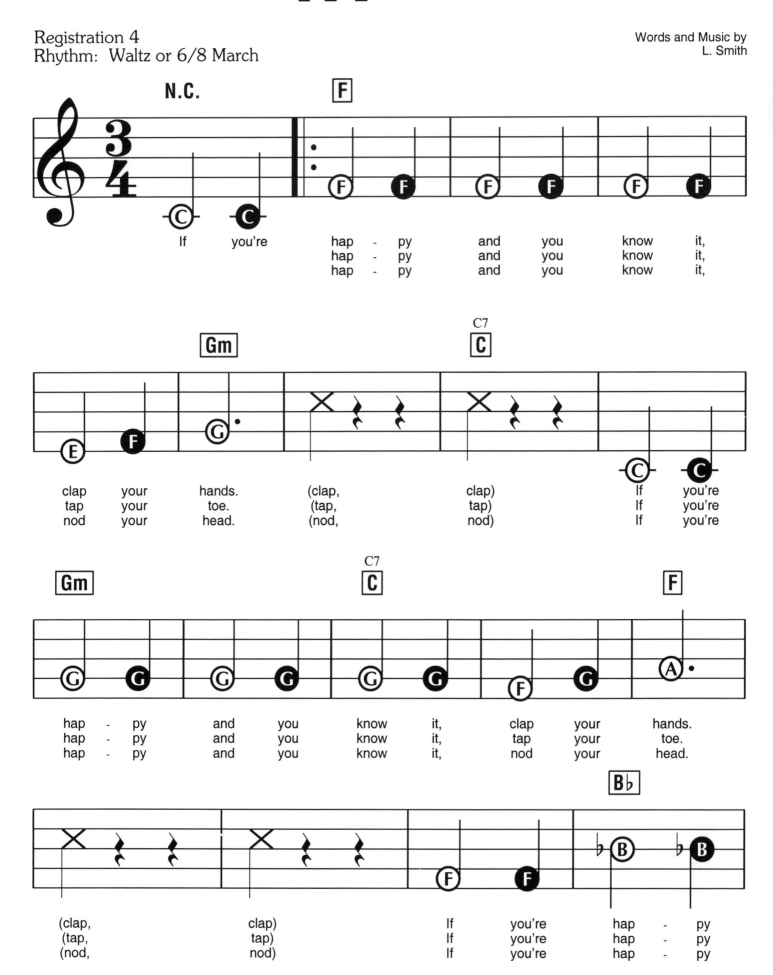

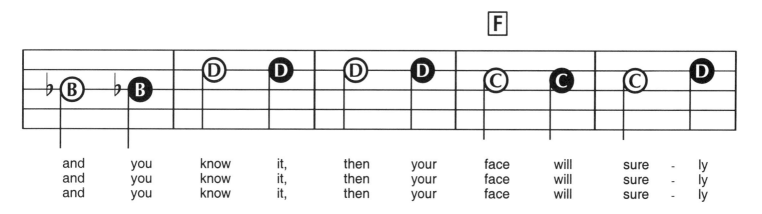

F

and   you   know   it,   then   your   face   will   sure - ly
and   you   know   it,   then   your   face   will   sure - ly
and   you   know   it,   then   your   face   will   sure - ly

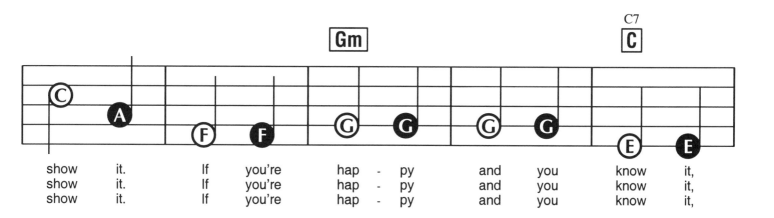

Gm   C7 C

show   it.   If   you're   hap - py   and   you   know   it,
show   it.   If   you're   hap - py   and   you   know   it,
show   it.   If   you're   hap - py   and   you   know   it,

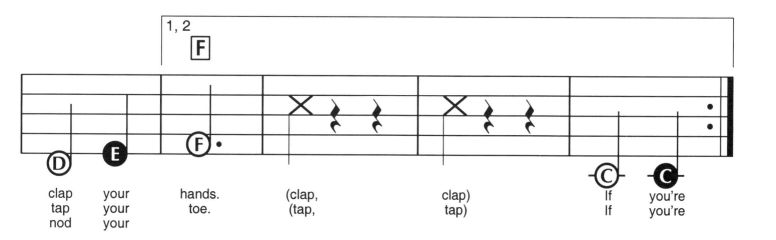

1, 2
F

clap   your   hands.   (clap,   clap)   If   you're
tap   your   toe.   (tap,   tap)   If   you're
nod   your   head.

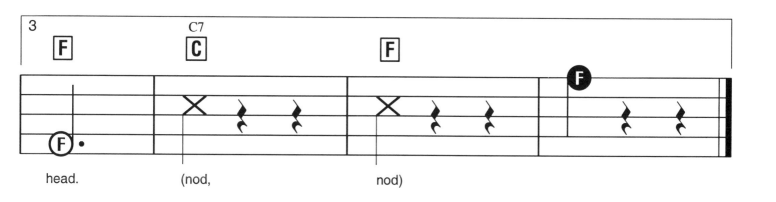

3
F   C7 C   F   F

head.   (nod,   nod)

Jacob's Ladder

Registration 1
Rhythm: Waltz

African-American Spiritual

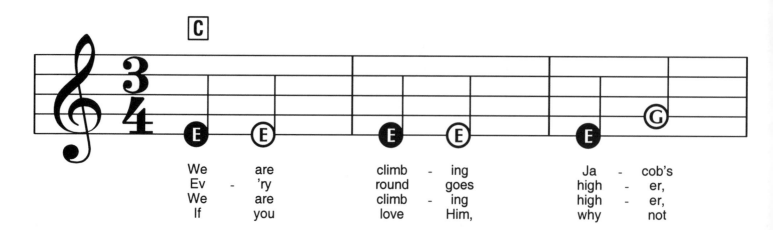

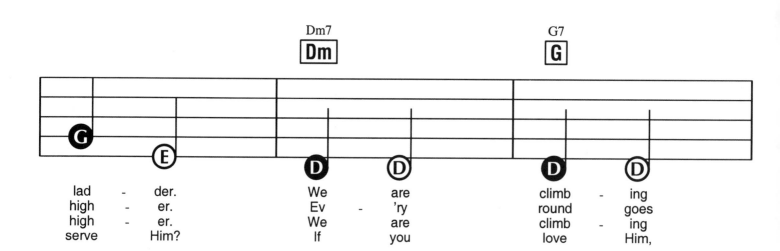

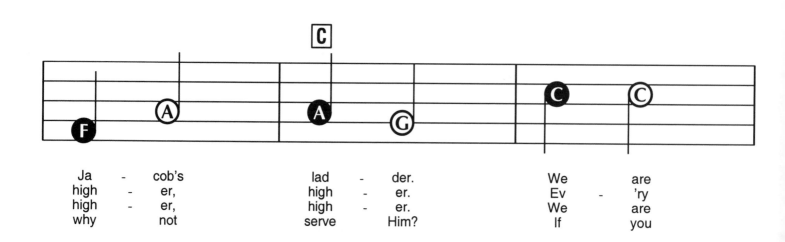

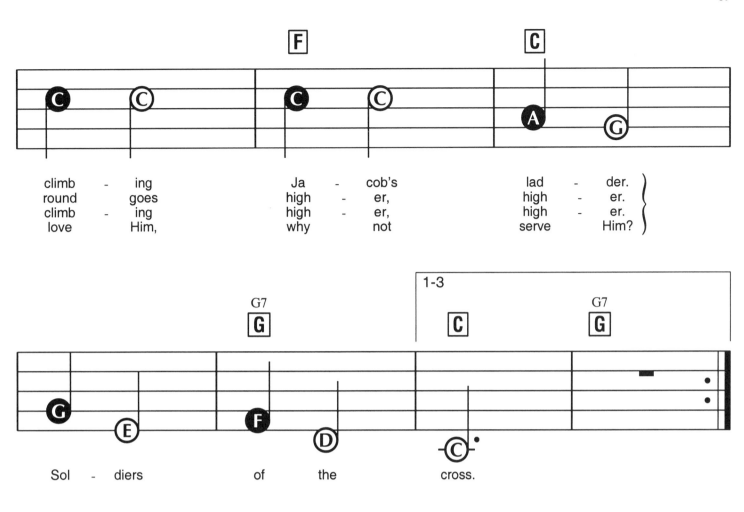

climb - ing
round goes
climb - ing
love Him,

F

Ja - cob's
high - er,
high - er,
why not

C

lad - der.
high - er.
high - er.
serve Him?

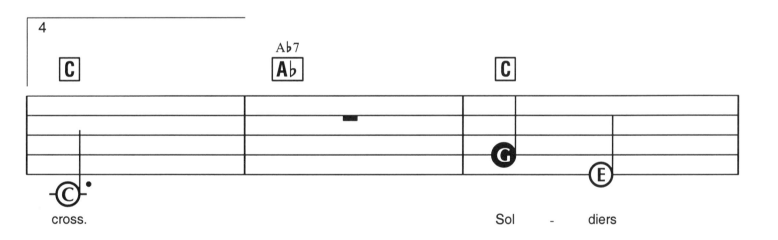

G7
G

1-3

C

G7
G

Sol - diers of the cross.

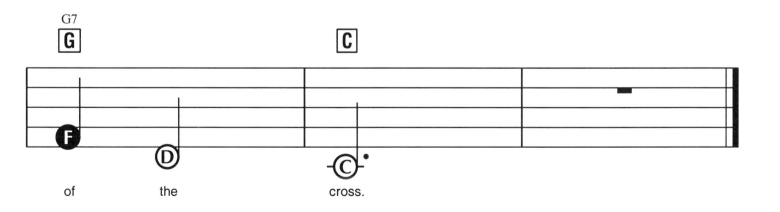

4

C

Ab7
Ab

C

cross.

Sol - diers

G7
G

C

of the cross.

Jesus in the Morning

Registration 10
Rhythm: Gospel or Shuffle

Traditional

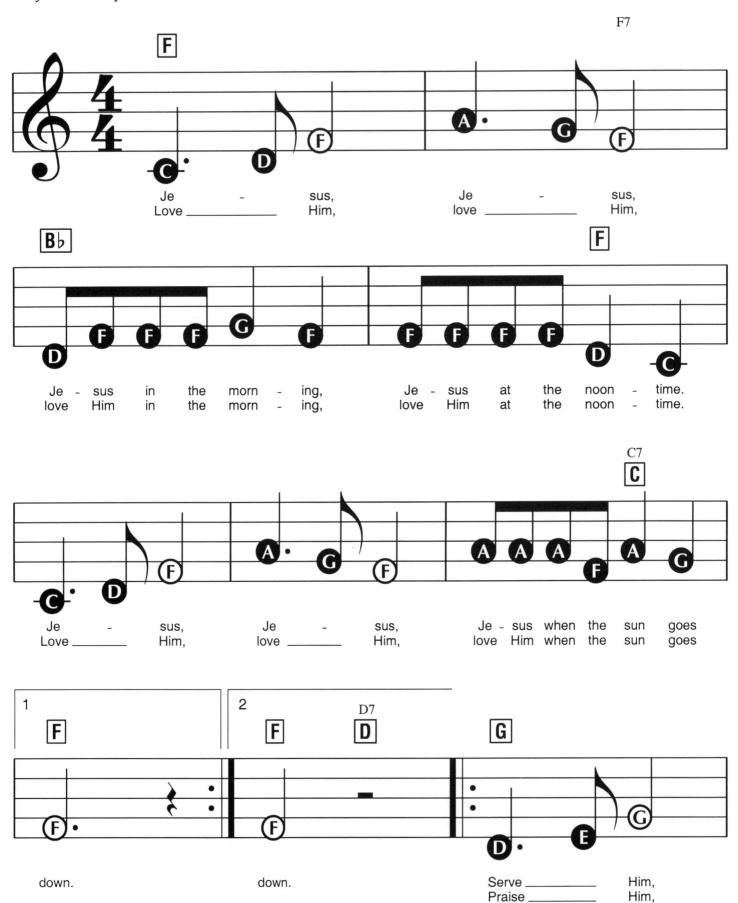

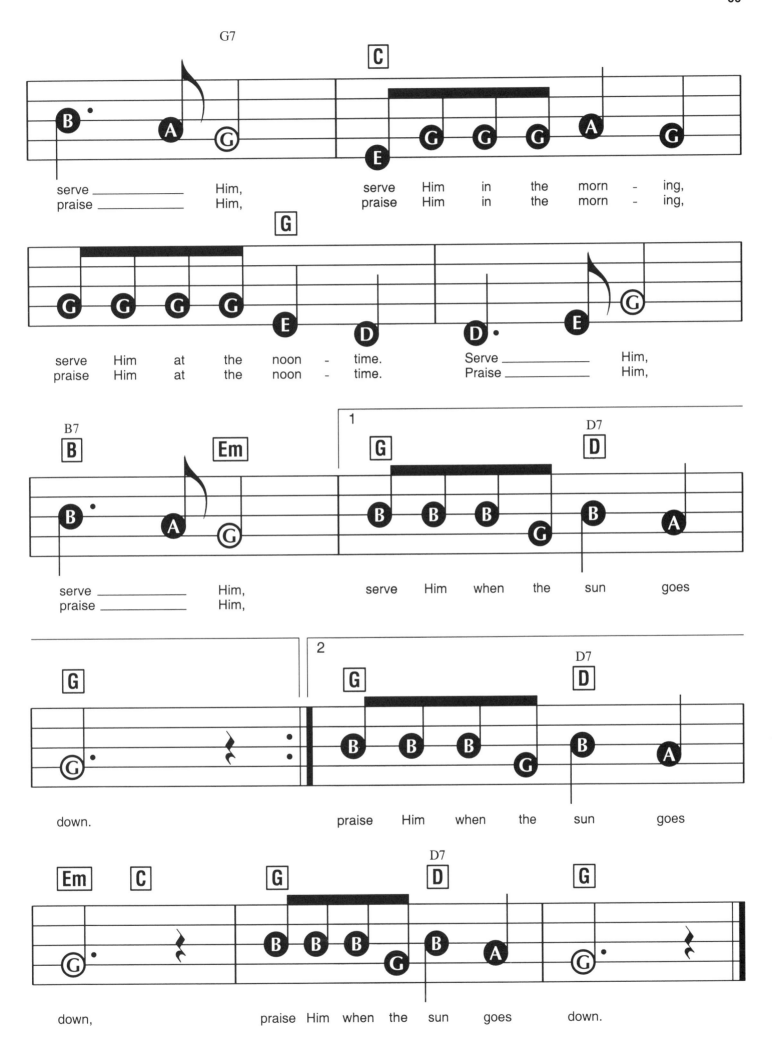

Jesus Loves Even Me
(I Am So Glad)

Registration 1
Rhythm: Waltz

Words and Music by
Philip P. Bliss

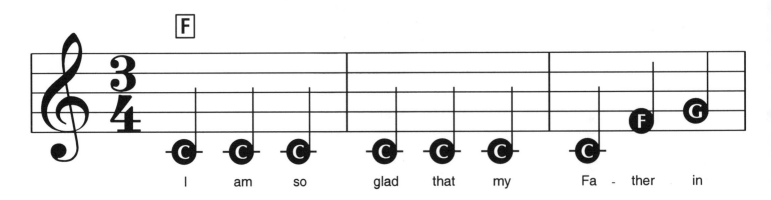

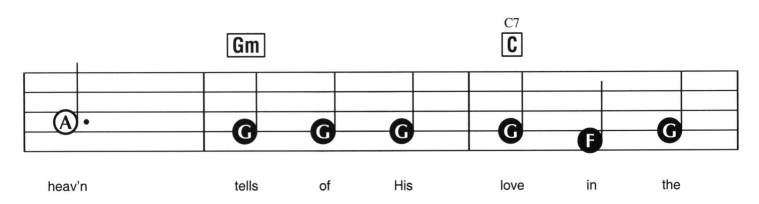

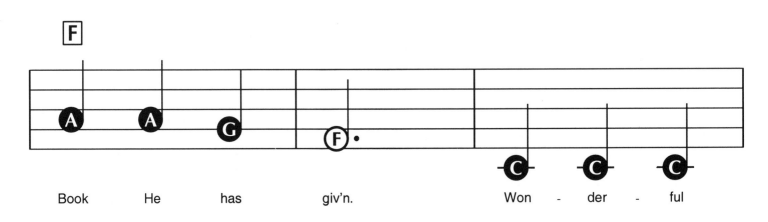

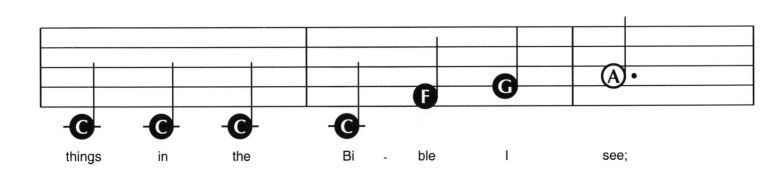

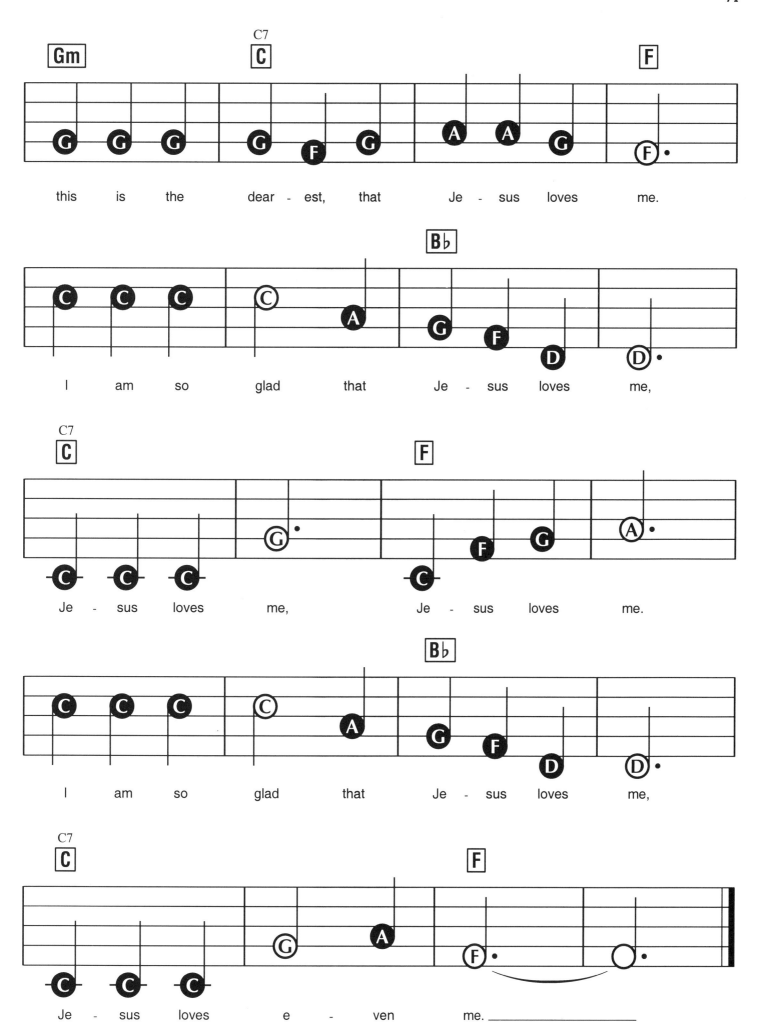

Jesus Loves Me

Registration 2
Rhythm: Swing

Words by Anna B. Warner
Music by William B. Bradbury

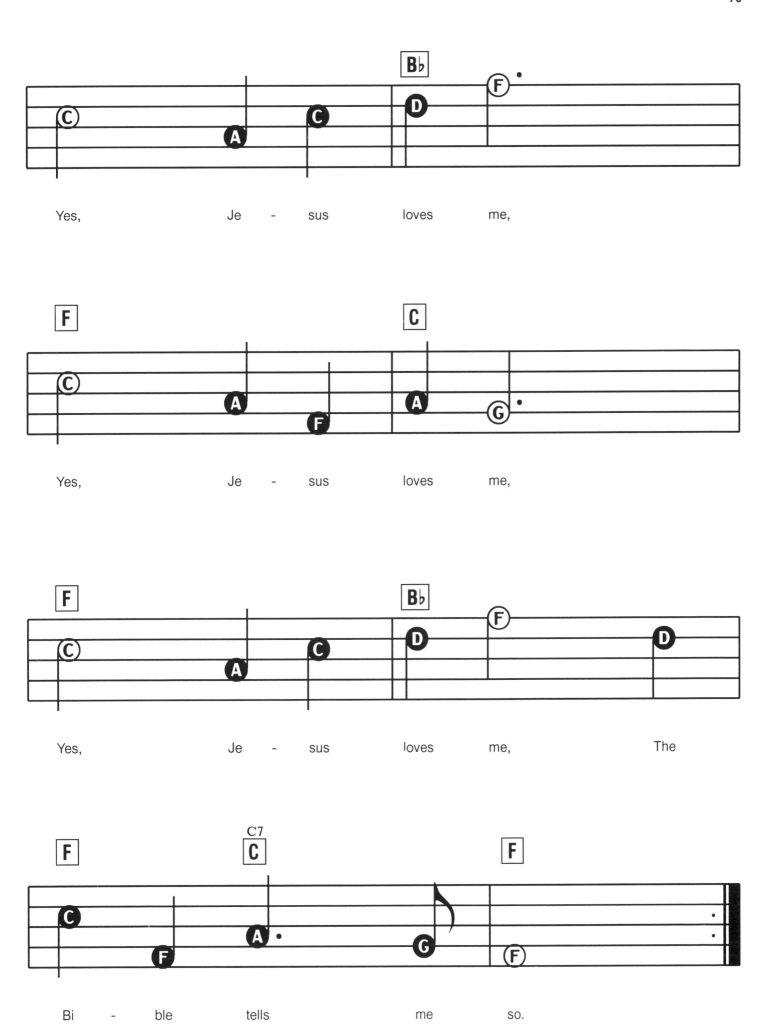

Jesus Loves the Little Children

Registration 4
Rhythm: Country or Swing

Words by Rev. C.H. Woolston
Music by George F. Root

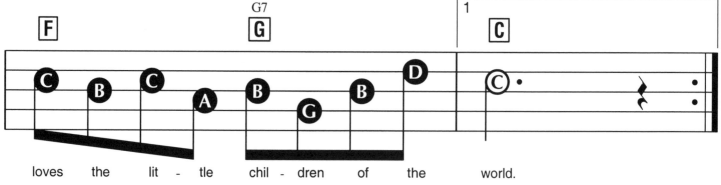

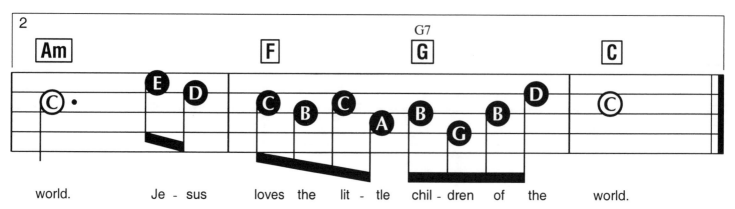

Rock-A-My Soul

Registration 9
Rhythm: Rock or 8 Beat

African-American Spiritual

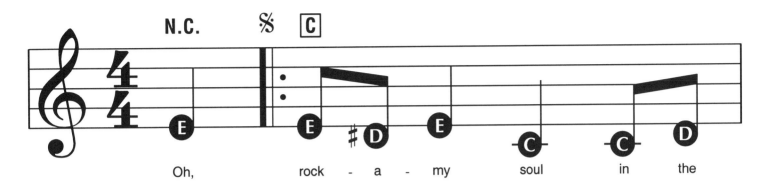

N.C. % **C**

Oh, rock - a - my soul in the

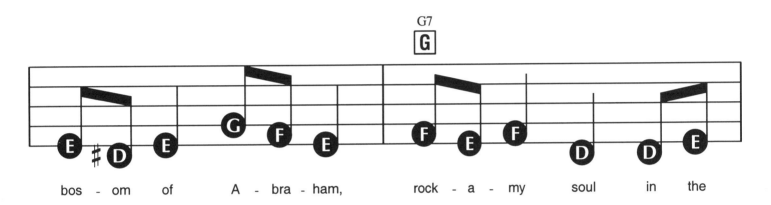

G7
G

bos - om of A - bra - ham, rock - a - my soul in the

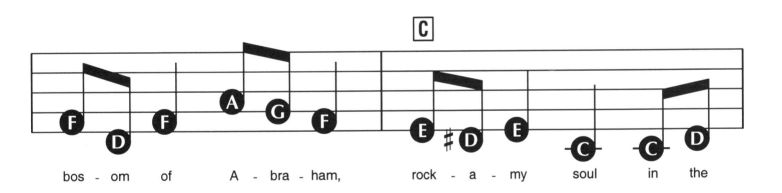

C

bos - om of A - bra - ham, rock - a - my soul in the

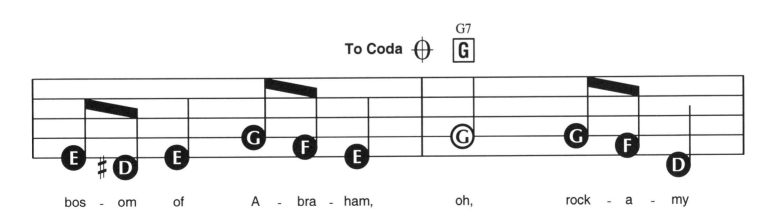

To Coda ⊕ G7 **G**

bos - om of A - bra - ham, oh, rock - a - my

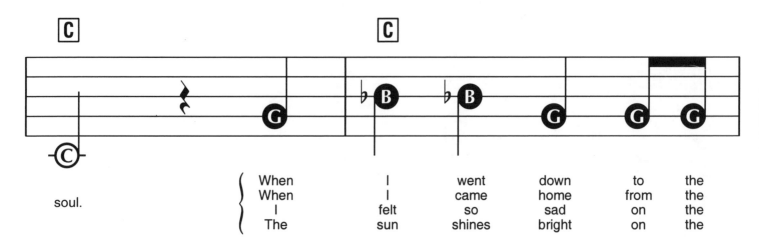

C

C

soul.

When I went down to the
When I came home from the
I felt so sad on the
The sun shines bright on the

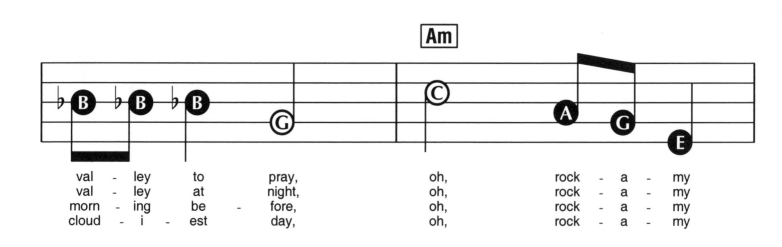

Am

val - ley to pray, oh, rock - a - my
val - ley at night, oh, rock - a - my
morn - ing be - fore, oh, rock - a - my
cloud - i - est day, oh, rock - a - my

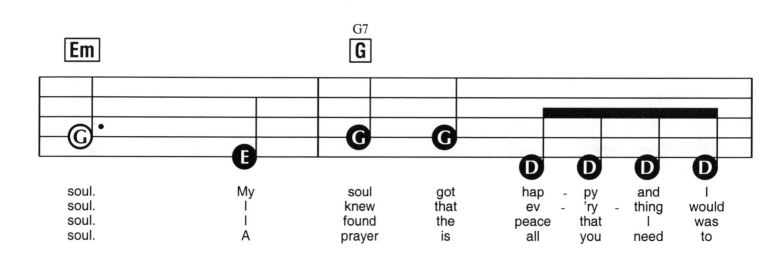

Em

G7
G

soul. My soul got hap - py and I
soul. I knew that the ev - 'ry - thing would
soul. I found peace that I was
soul. A prayer is all you need to

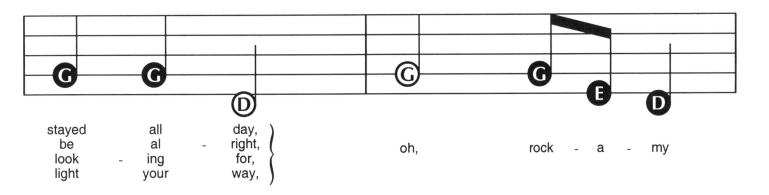

stayed   all   day,
be   al - right,   oh,   rock - a - my
look - ing   for,
light   your   way,

1-3

4

D.S. al Coda
(Return to 𝄋
Play to ⊕ and
Skip to Coda)

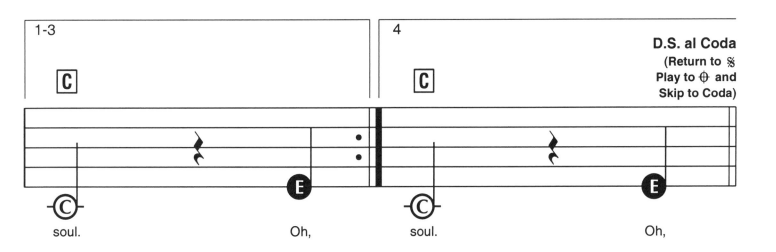

soul.   Oh,   soul.   Oh,

CODA   G7

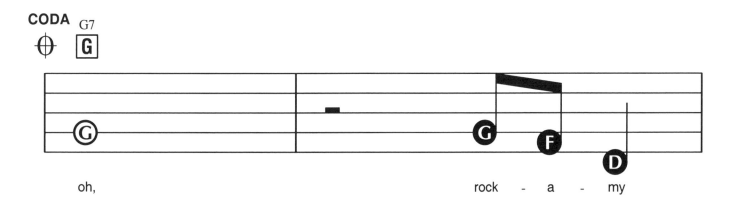

oh,   rock - a - my

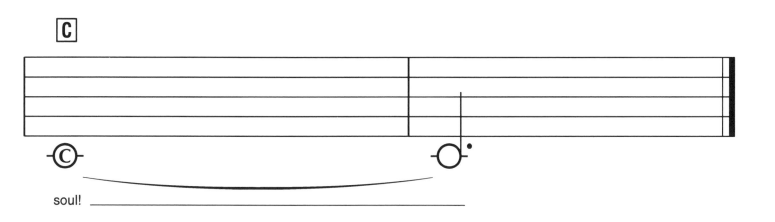

soul!

Joshua
(Fit the Battle of Jericho)

Registration 6
Rhythm: Swing

African-American Spiritual

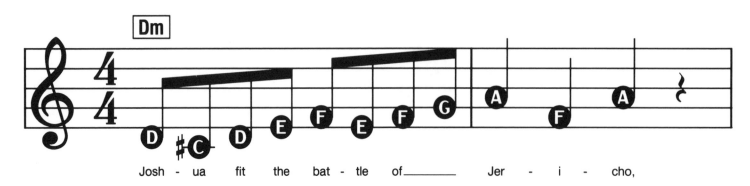

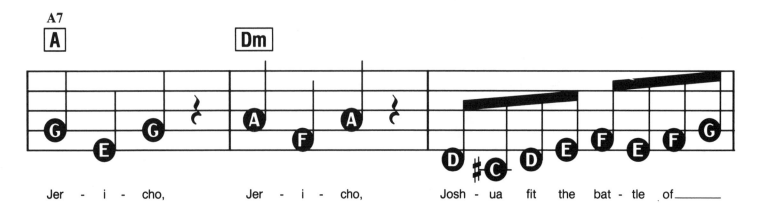

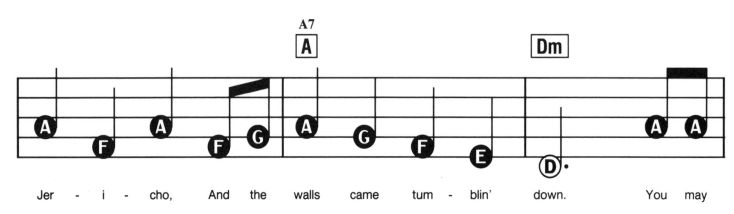

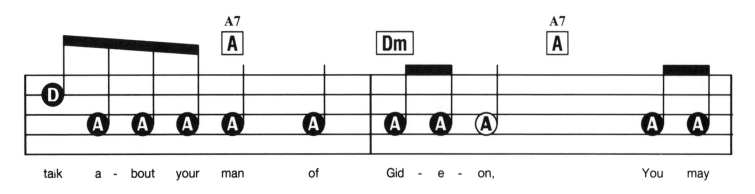

79

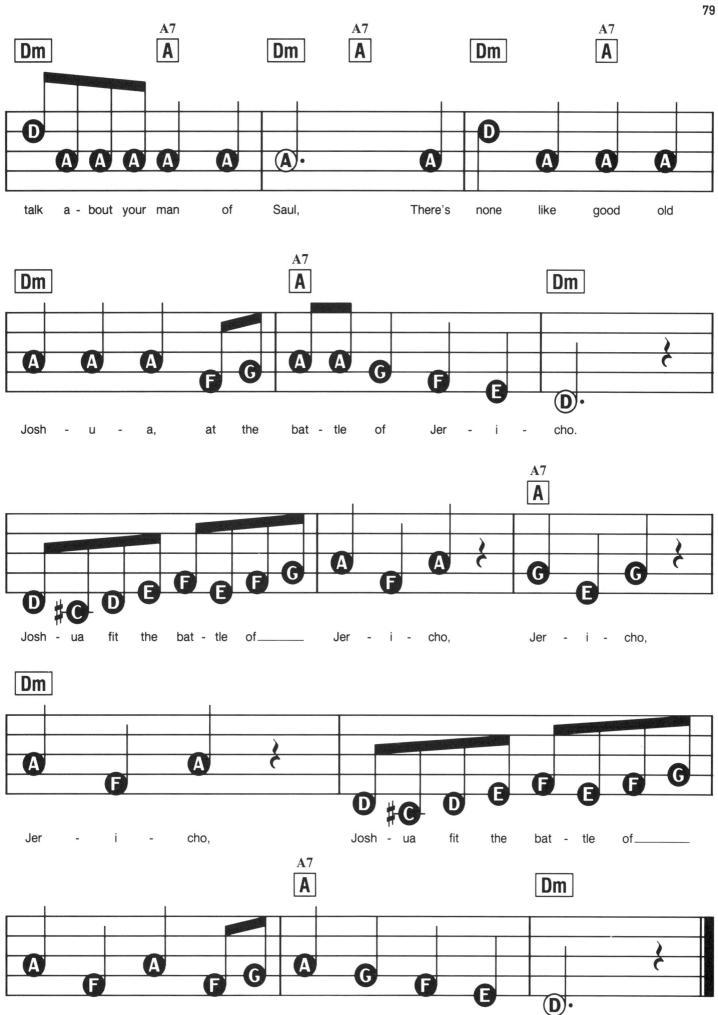

Kum Ba Yah

Registration 3
Rhythm: 8 Beat or Rock

Traditional Spiritual

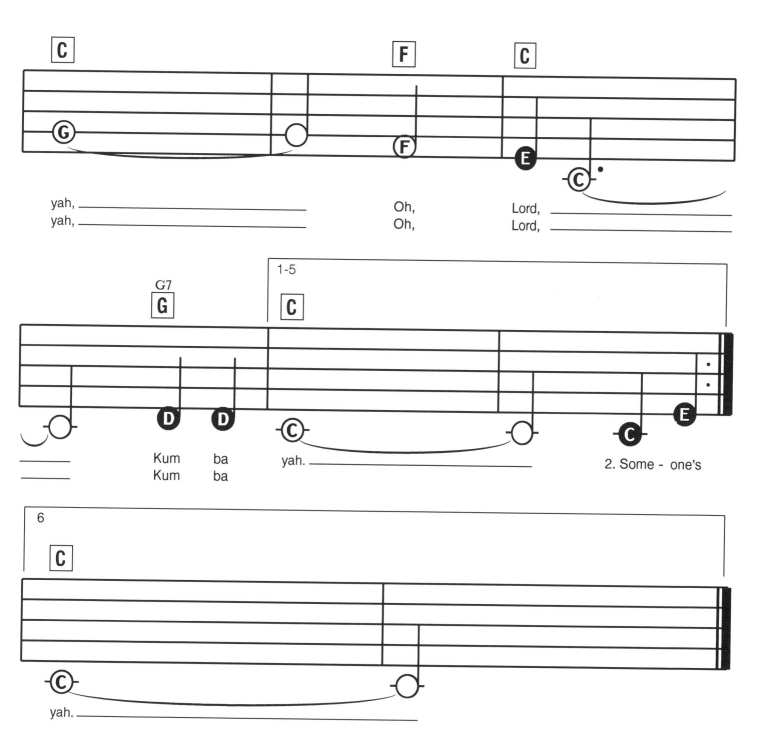

Additional Lyrics

3. Someone's singin', Lord, Kum ba yah...
4. Someone's cryin', Lord, Kum ba yah...
5. Someone's dancin', Lord, Kum ba yah...
6. Someone's shoutin', Lord, Kum ba yah...

Little David, Play on Your Harp

Registration 8
Rhythm: Gospel or Fox Trot

Traditional

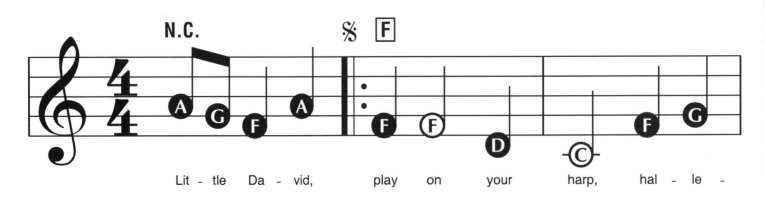

Lit - tle Da - vid, play on your harp, hal - le -

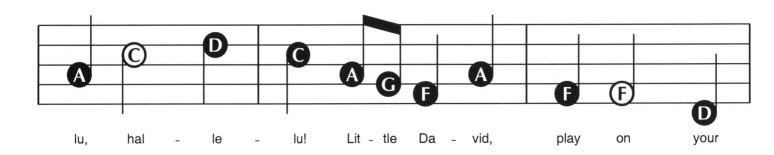

lu, hal - le - lu! Lit - tle Da - vid, play on your

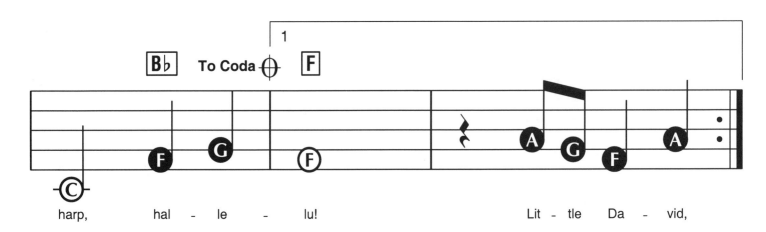

harp, hal - le - lu! Lit - tle Da - vid,

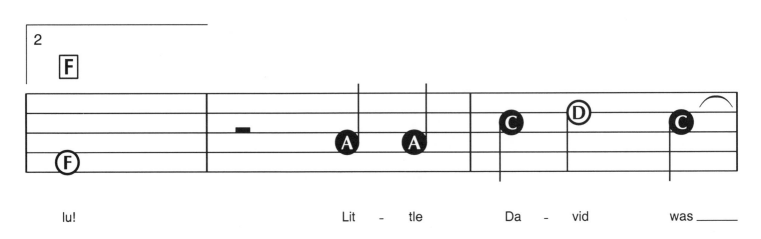

lu! Lit - tle Da - vid was ____

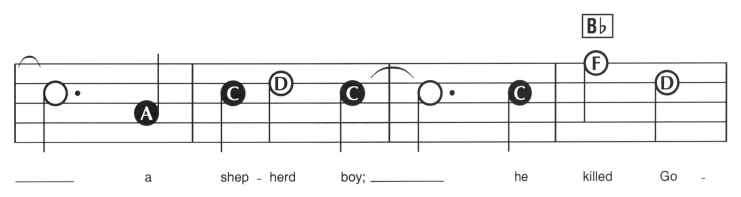

a   shep - herd   boy; _____   he   killed   Go -

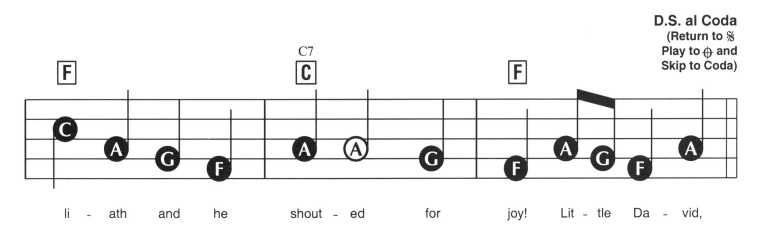

D.S. al Coda
(Return to 𝄋
Play to ⊕ and
Skip to Coda)

li - ath   and   he   shout - ed   for   joy!   Lit - tle   Da - vid,

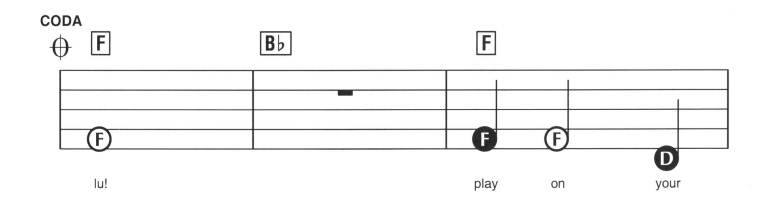

CODA

lu!   play   on   your

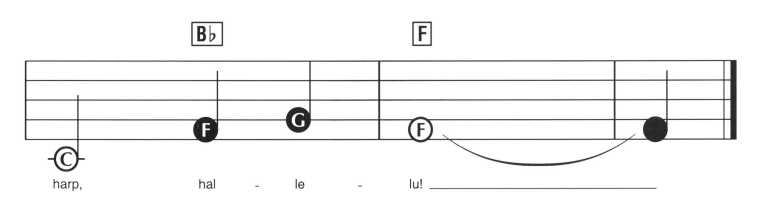

harp,   hal - le - lu! _____

Lord, I Want to Be a Christian

Registration 1
Rhythm: Gospel or Ballad

Traditional Spiritual

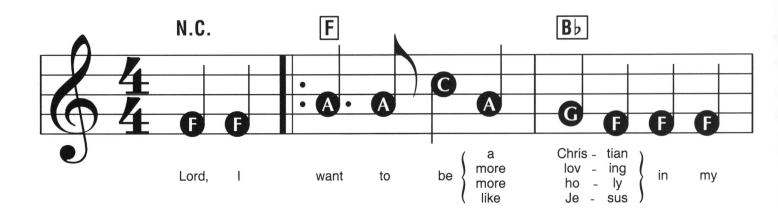

Lord, I want to be { a Christian / more lov - ing / more ho - ly / like Je - sus } in my

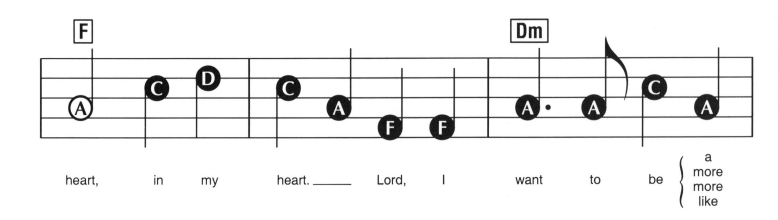

heart, in my heart. _____ Lord, I want to be { a / more / more / like }

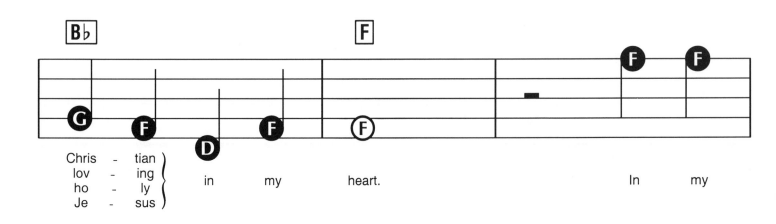

Chris - tian / lov - ing / ho - ly / Je - sus } in my heart. In my

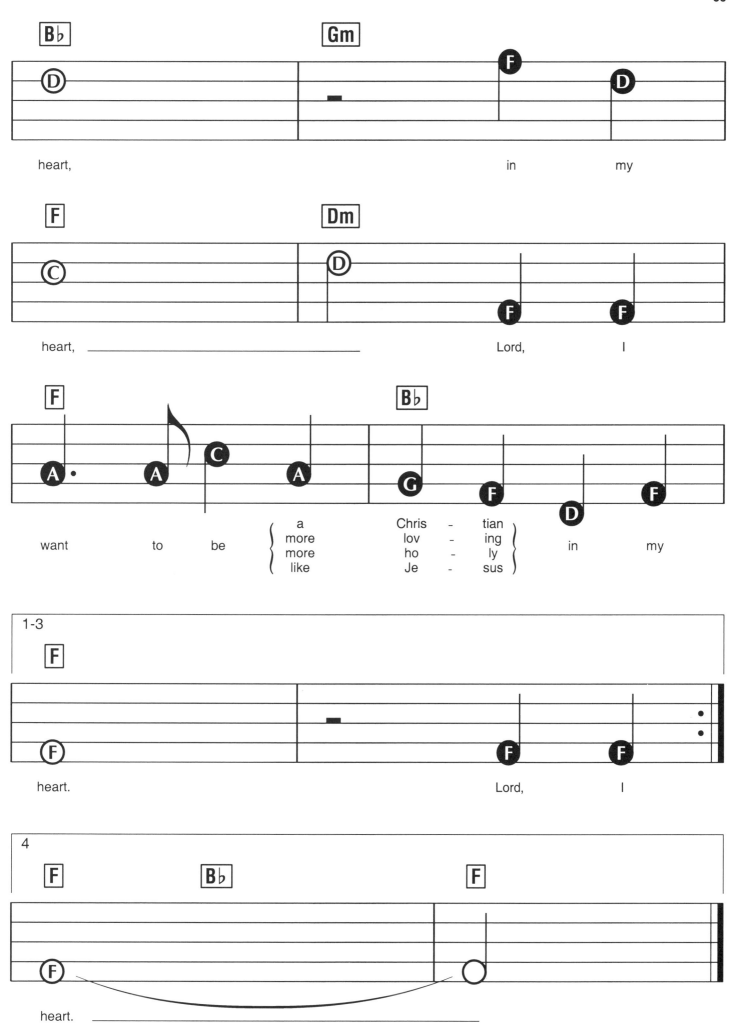

My God Is So Great, So Strong and So Mighty

Registration 8
Rhythm: Waltz or 6/8 March

Traditional

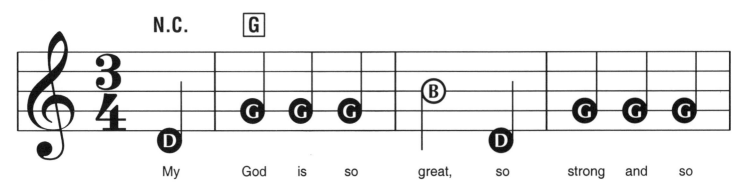

My God is so great, so strong and so

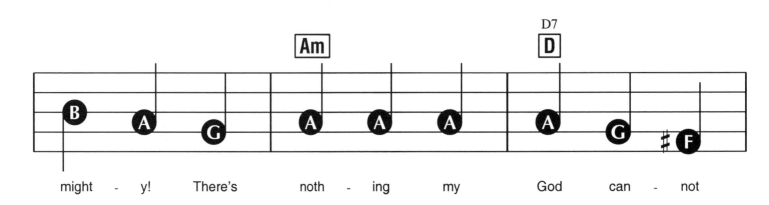

might - y! There's noth - ing my God can - not

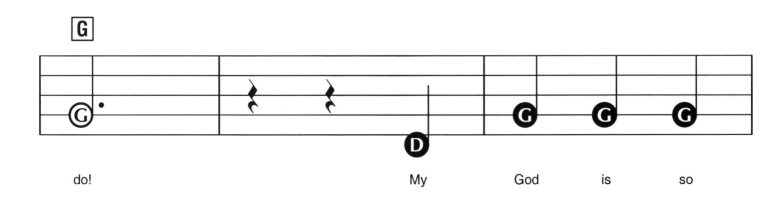

do! My God is so

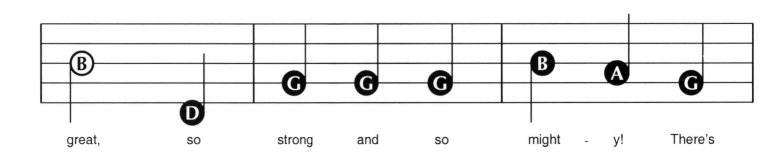

great, so strong and so might - y! There's

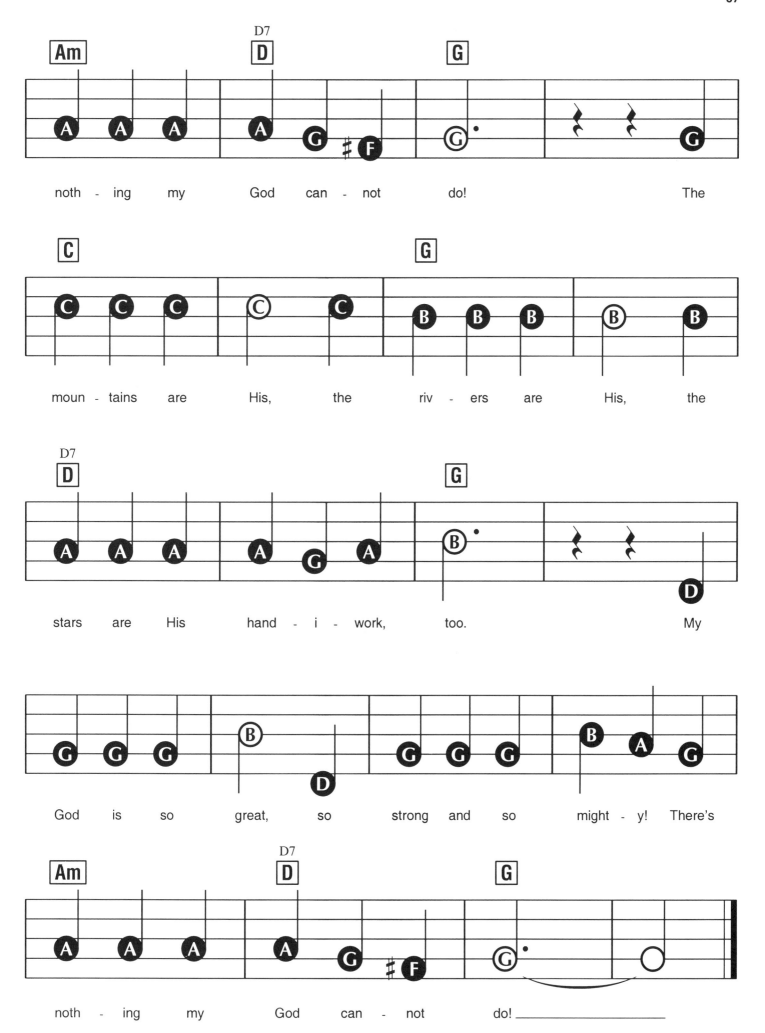

Nothing But the Blood

Registration 2
Rhythm: Ballad or Fox Trot

Words and Music by
Robert Lowry

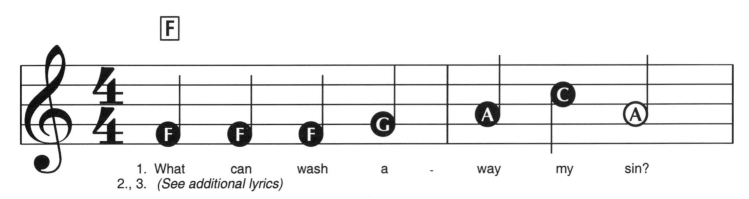

1. What can wash a - way my sin?
2., 3. *(See additional lyrics)*

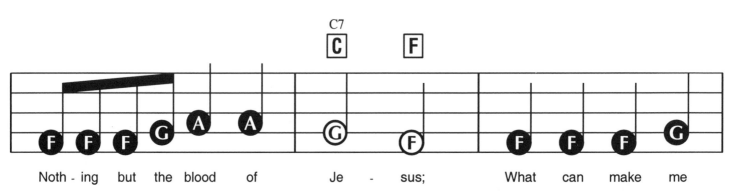

Noth - ing but the blood of Je - sus; What can make me

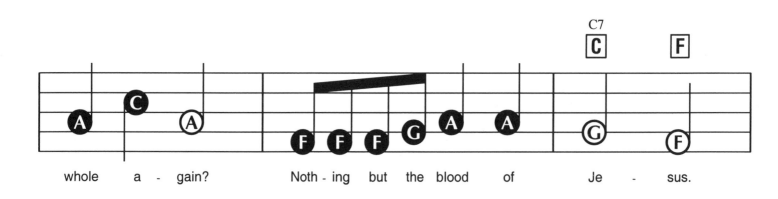

whole a - gain? Noth - ing but the blood of Je - sus.

Refrain

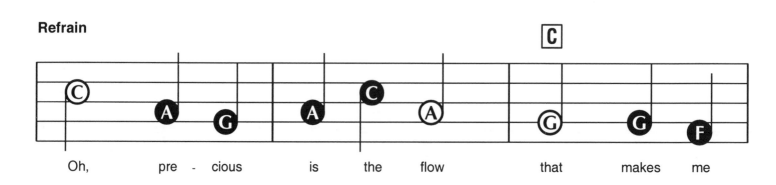

Oh, pre - cious is the flow that makes me

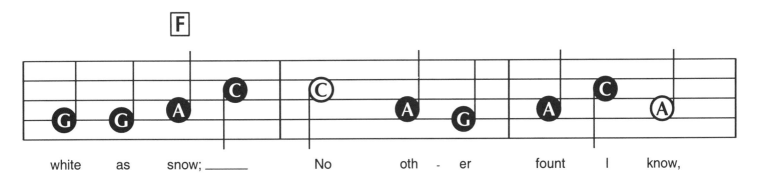

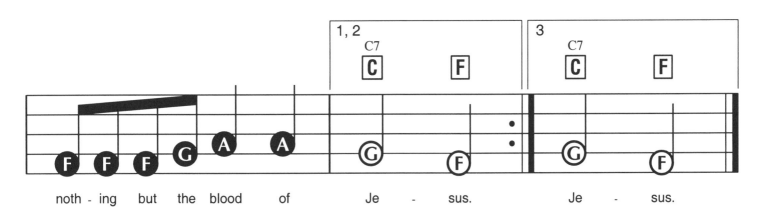

Additional Lyrics

2. For my pardon this I see
   Nothing but the blood of Jesus;
   For my cleansing this my plea
   Nothing but the blood of Jesus.
   Refrain

3. Nothing can for sin atone
   Nothing but the blood of Jesus;
   Naught of good that I have done
   Nothing but the blood of Jesus.
   Refrain

Oh, Be Careful

Registration 8
Rhythm: March

Traditional

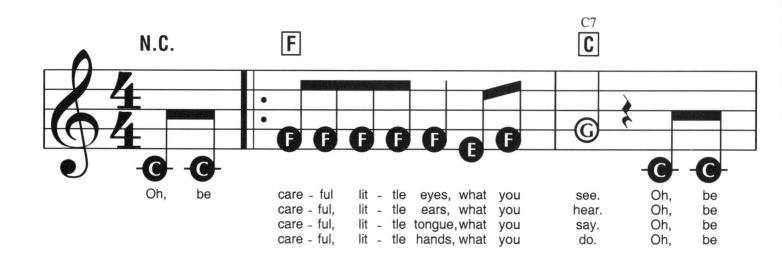

Oh,   be   care - ful   lit - tle eyes, what you   see.   Oh, be
                care - ful,   lit - tle ears, what you   hear.   Oh, be
                care - ful,   lit - tle tongue, what you   say.   Oh, be
                care - ful,   lit - tle hands, what you   do.   Oh, be

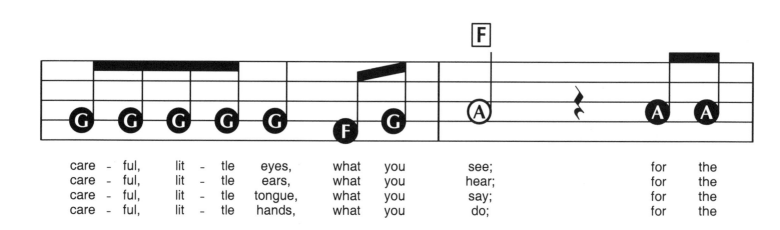

care - ful,   lit - tle eyes,   what you   see;   for the
care - ful,   lit - tle ears,   what you   hear;   for the
care - ful,   lit - tle tongue, what you   say;   for the
care - ful,   lit - tle hands, what you   do;   for the

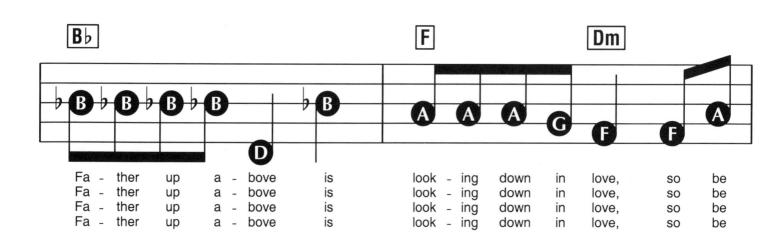

Fa - ther up   a - bove is   look - ing down in love,   so be
Fa - ther up   a - bove is   look - ing down in love,   so be
Fa - ther up   a - bove is   look - ing down in love,   so be
Fa - ther up   a - bove is   look - ing down in love,   so be

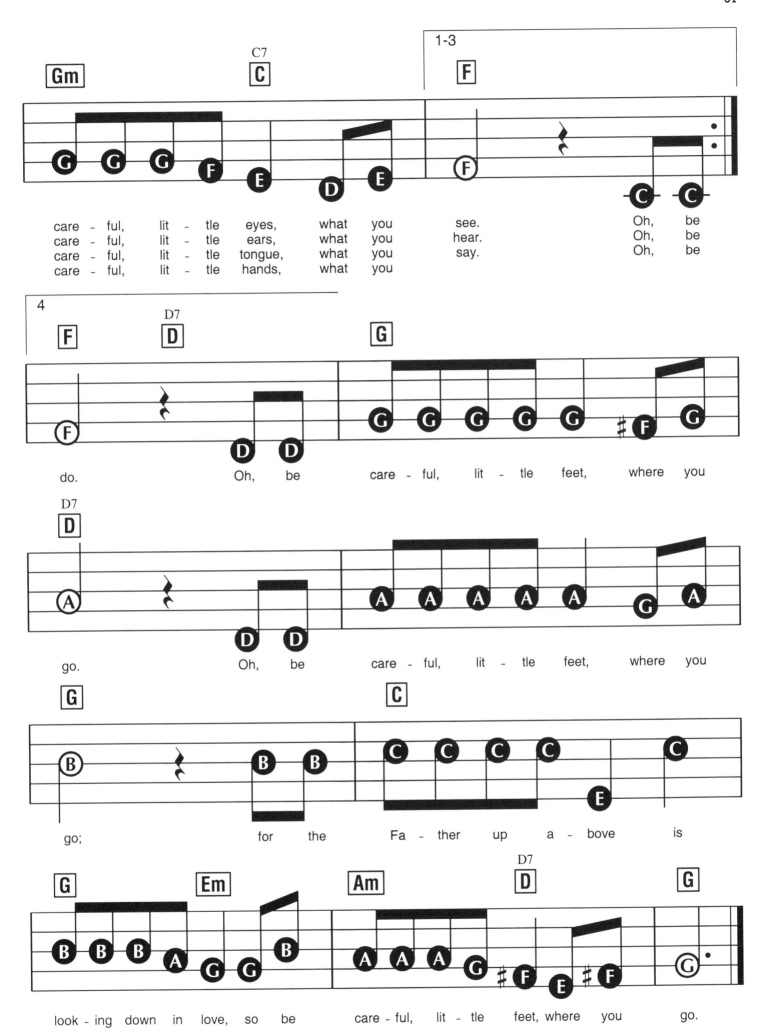

Oh, How I Love Jesus

Registration 2
Rhythm: 6/8 March or Waltz

Words by Frederick Whitfield
Traditional American Melody

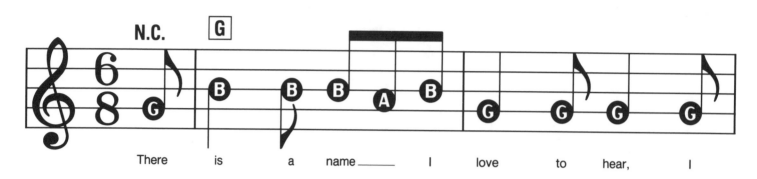

There is a name ___ I love to hear, I

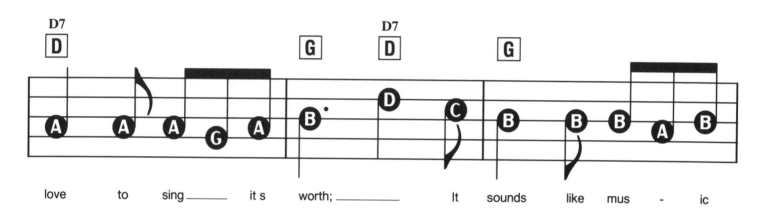

love to sing ___ it s worth; ___ It sounds like mus - ic

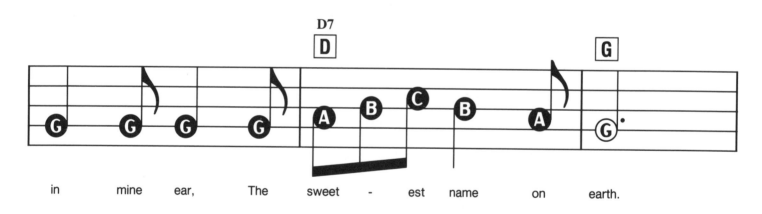

in mine ear, The sweet - est name on earth.

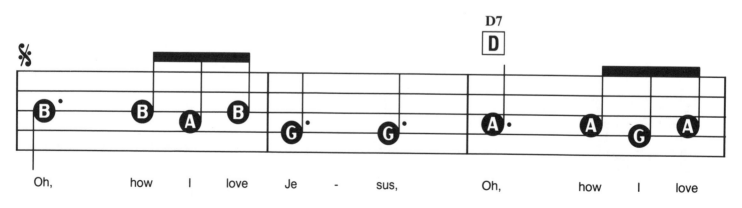

Oh, how I love Je - sus, Oh, how I love

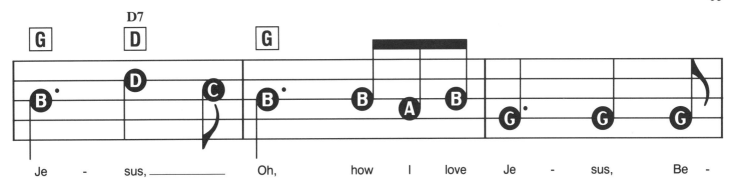

Je - sus, _____ Oh, how I love Je - sus, Be -

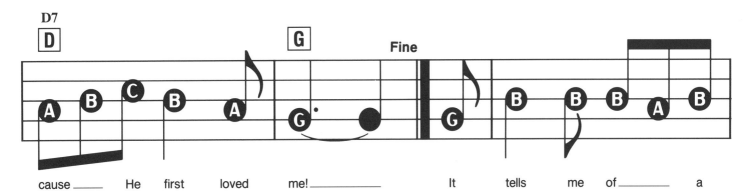

cause _____ He first loved me! _____ It tells me of _____ a

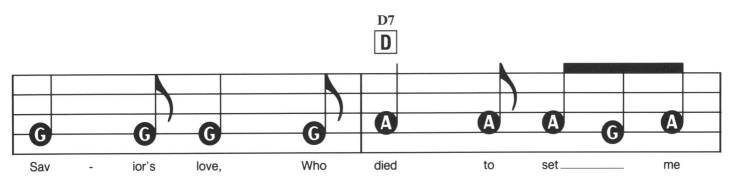

Sav - ior's love, Who died to set _____ me

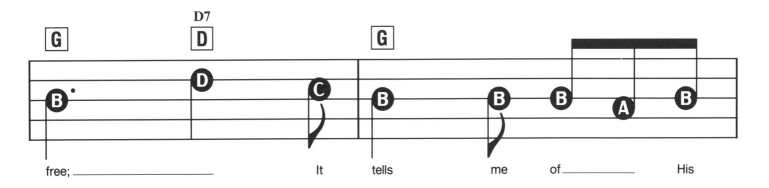

free; _____ It tells me of _____ His

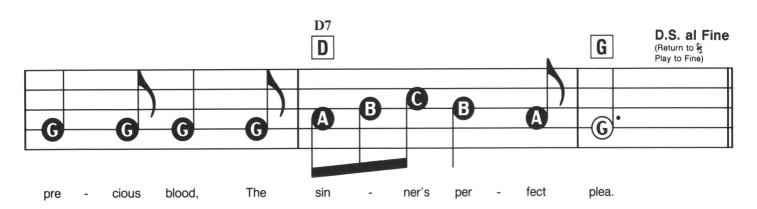

pre - cious blood, The sin - ner's per - fect plea.

Praise Him, All Ye Little Children

Registration 8
Rhythm: 8 Beat or Country

Traditional Words
Music by Carey Bonner

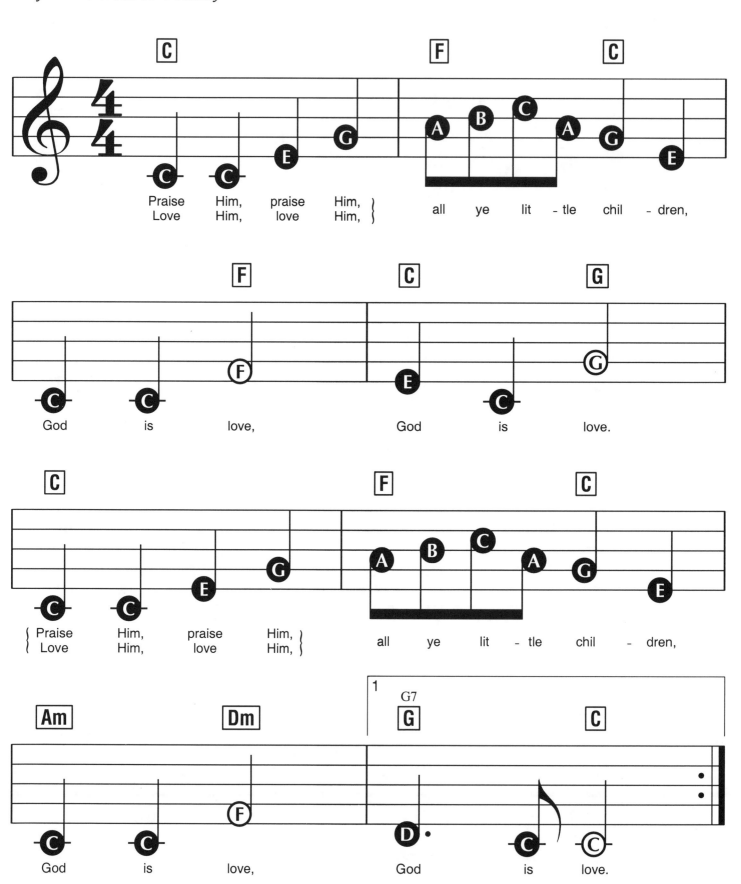

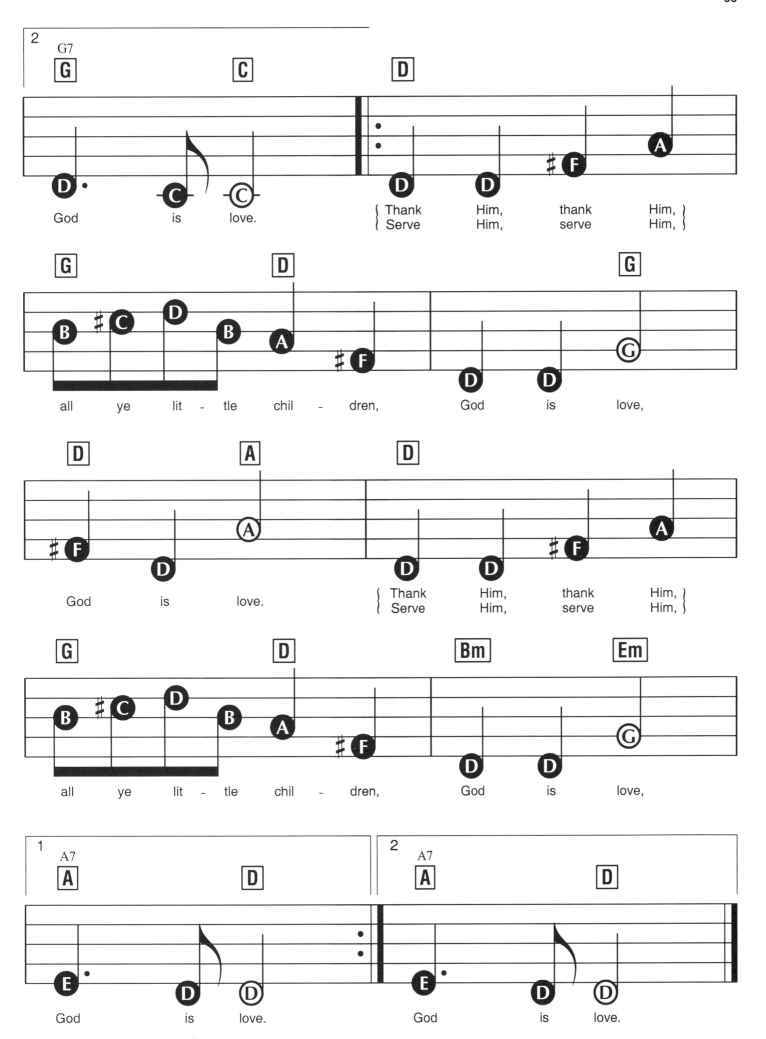

Simple Gifts

Registration 8
Rhythm: Fox Trot

Traditional Shaker Hymn

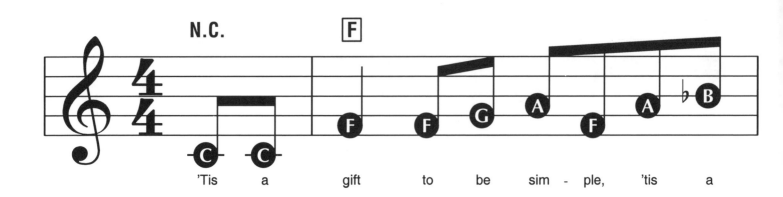

'Tis a   gift   to   be   sim - ple,   'tis   a

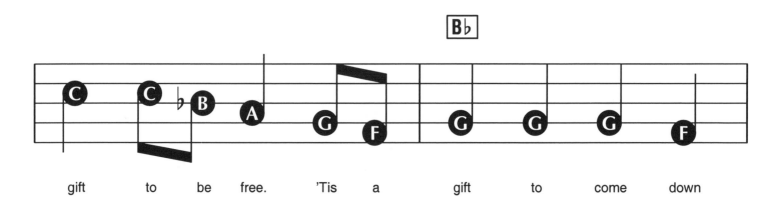

gift   to   be   free.   'Tis   a   gift   to   come   down

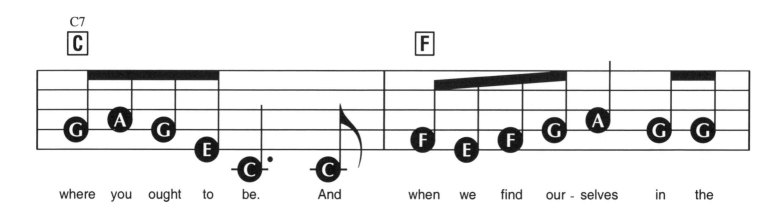

where   you   ought   to   be.   And   when   we   find   our - selves   in   the

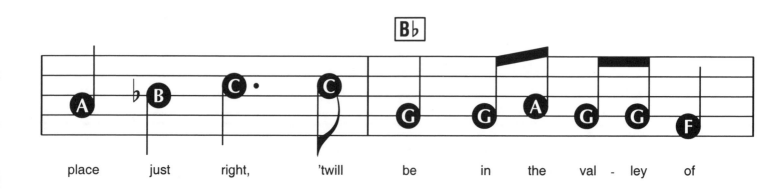

place   just   right,   'twill   be   in   the   val - ley   of

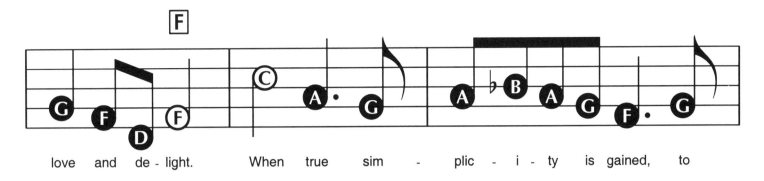

love and de- light. When true sim - plic - i - ty is gained, to

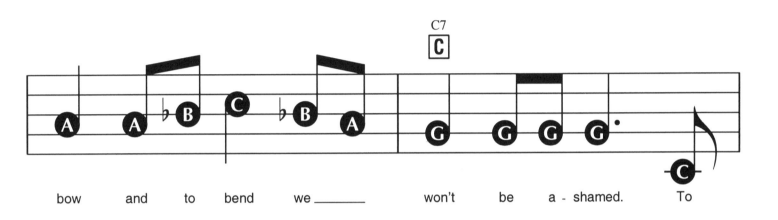

bow and to bend we _____ won't be a - shamed. To

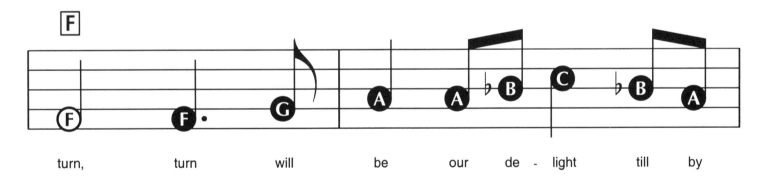

turn, turn will be our de - light till by

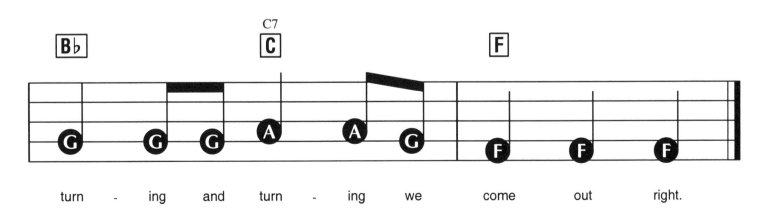

turn - ing and turn - ing we come out right.

Siyahamba
(We Are Marching in the Light of God)

Registration 5
Rhythm: Latin or 16 Beat

African Folksong

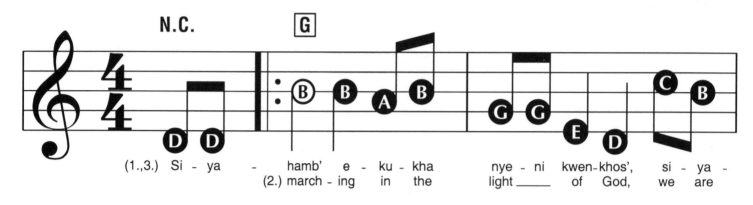

(1.,3.) Si - ya - hamb' e - ku - kha nye - ni kwen-khos', si - ya -
(2.) march - ing in the light _____ of God, we are

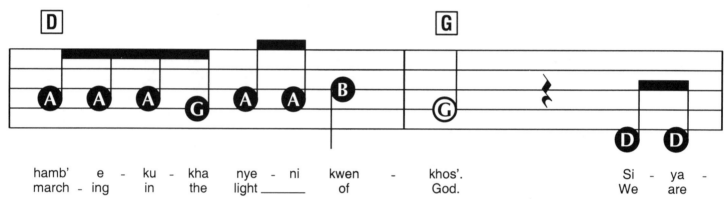

hamb' e - ku - kha nye - ni kwen - khos'. Si - ya -
march - ing in the light _____ of God. We are

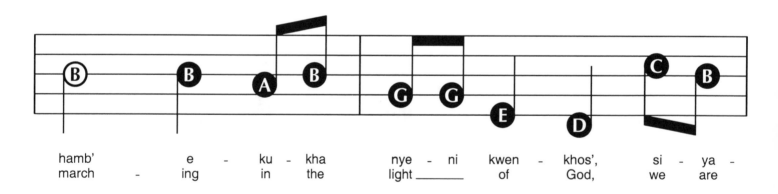

hamb' e - ku - kha nye - ni kwen - khos', si - ya -
march - ing in the light _____ of God, we are

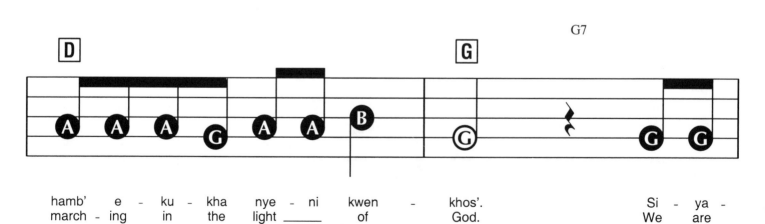

hamb' e - ku - kha nye - ni kwen - khos'. Si - ya -
march - ing in the light _____ of God. We are

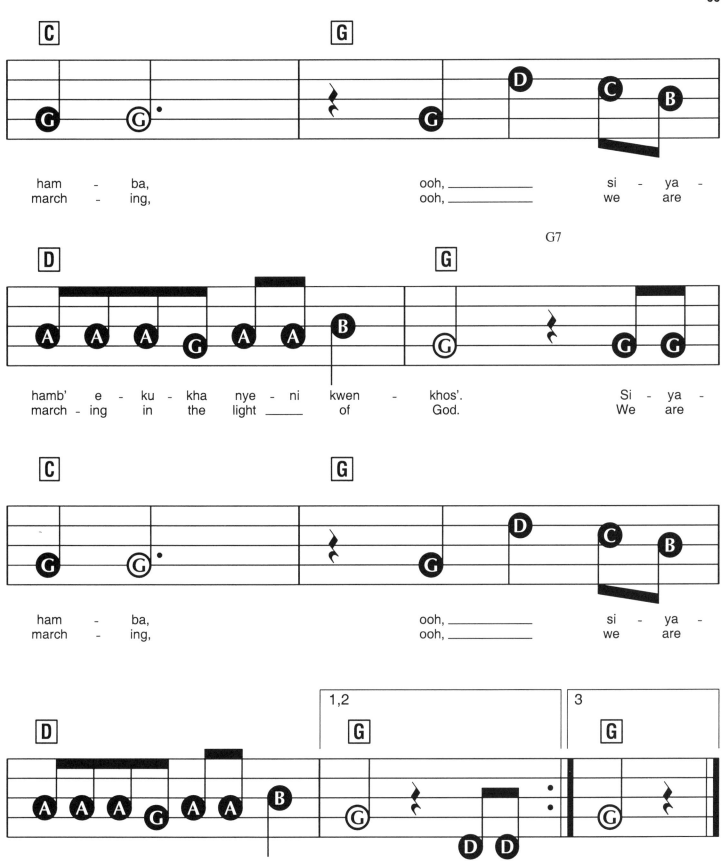

Pronunciation Guide

Siyahamba = see-ya-hahm-bah
Ekukha = eh-koo-kah
Nyeni = n yeh-nee
Kwenkhos' = kwehn-kōs

Standin' in the Need of Prayer

Registration 2
Rhythm: Swing

African-American Spiritual

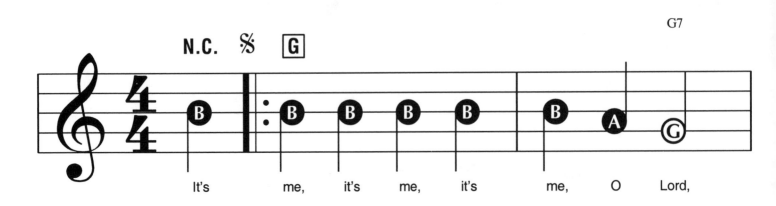

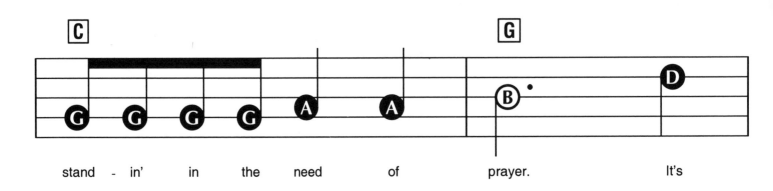

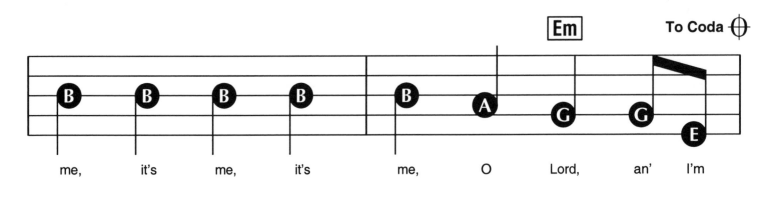

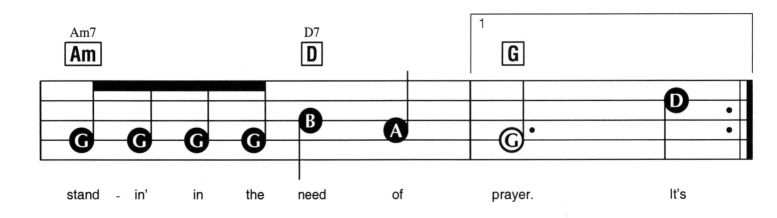

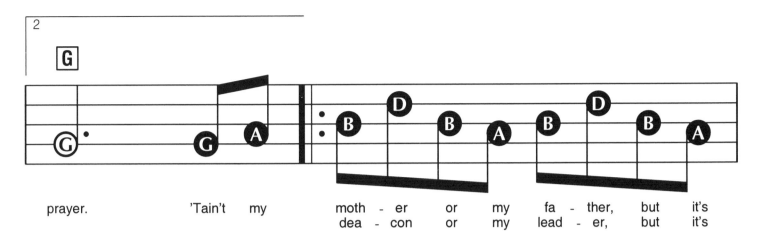

prayer.   'Tain't my   moth – er   or   my   fa – ther, but   it's
                         dea – con   or   my   lead – er, but   it's

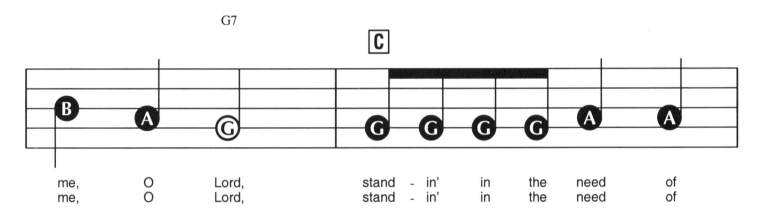

me,   O   Lord,   stand – in'   in   the   need   of
me,   O   Lord,   stand – in'   in   the   need   of

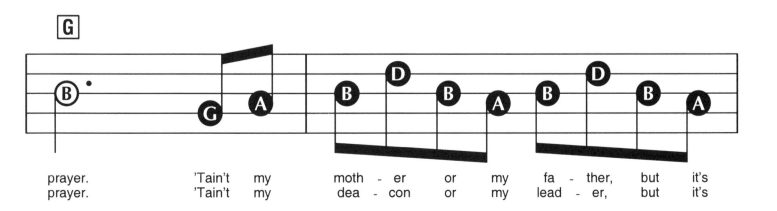

prayer.   'Tain't my   moth – er   or   my   fa – ther, but   it's
prayer.   'Tain't my   dea – con   or   my   lead – er, but   it's

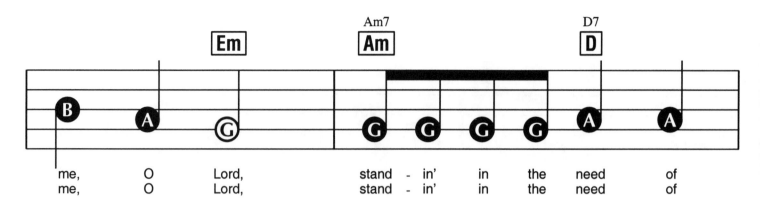

me,   O   Lord,   stand - in' in the need of
me,   O   Lord,   stand - in' in the need of

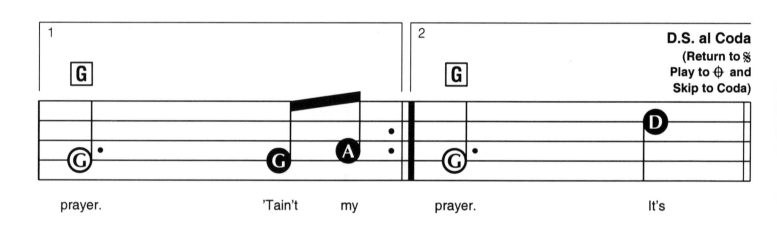

prayer.   'Tain't my   prayer.   It's

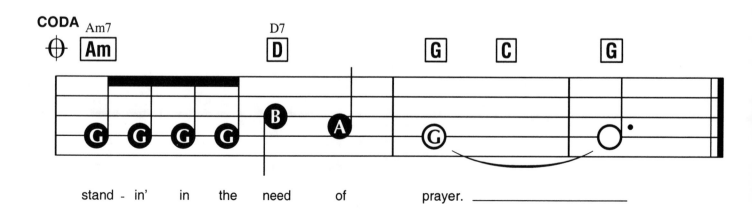

stand - in' in the need of   prayer. _____

Stop! And Let Me Tell You

Registration 7
Rhythm: March or Fox Trot

Traditional

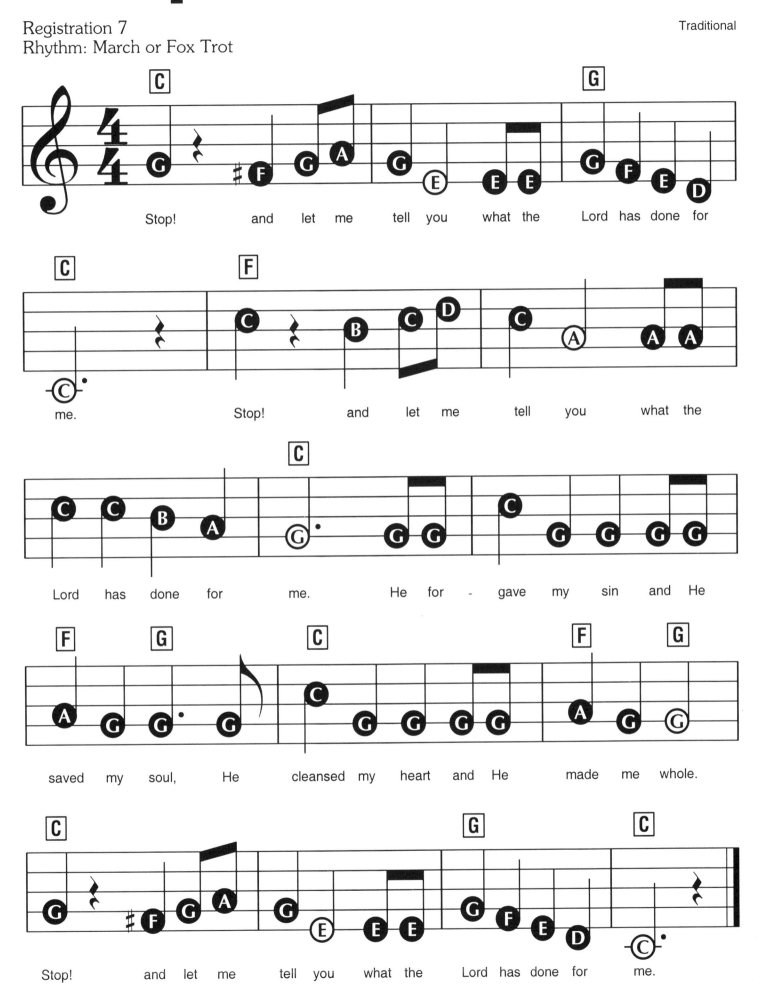

Tell Me the Stories of Jesus

Registration 8
Rhythm: Waltz or 6/8 March

Words by William H. Parker
Music by Frederic A. Challinor

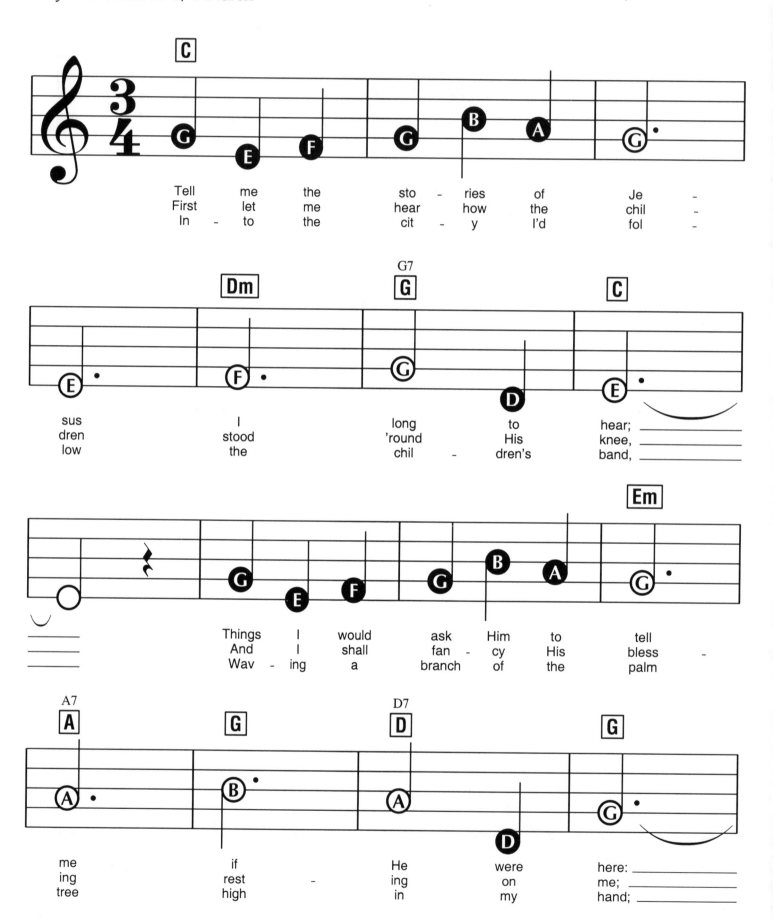

105

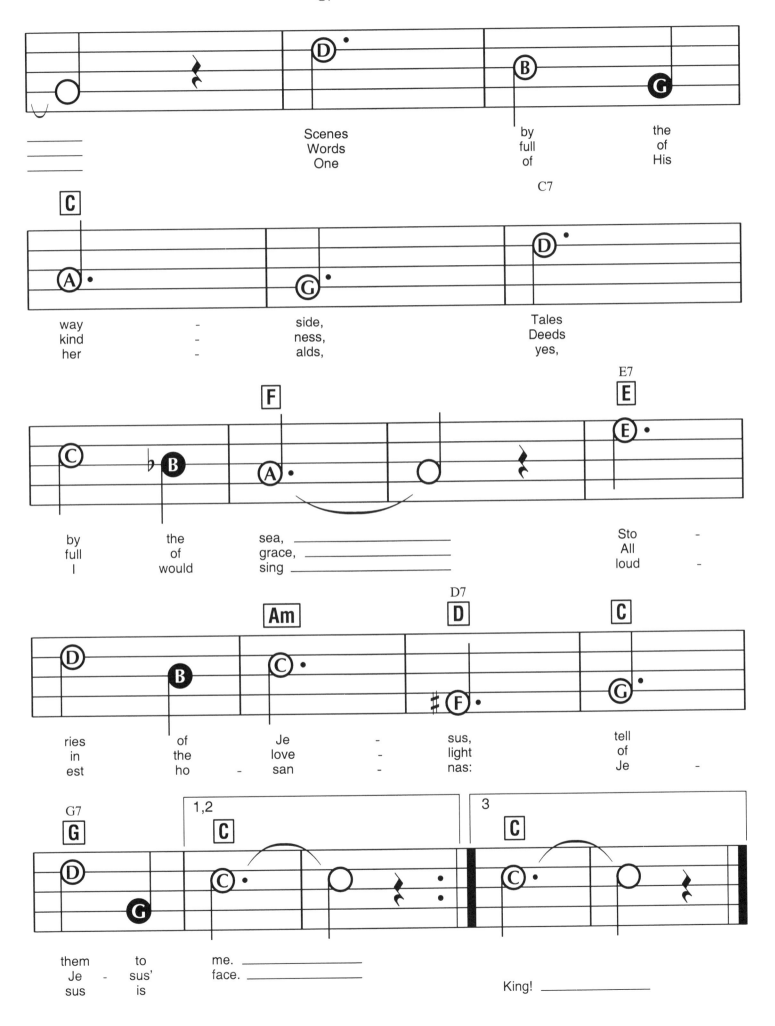

This Is My Father's World

Registration 8
Rhythm: Ballad or Country

Words by Maltbie Babcock
Music by Franklin L. Sheppard

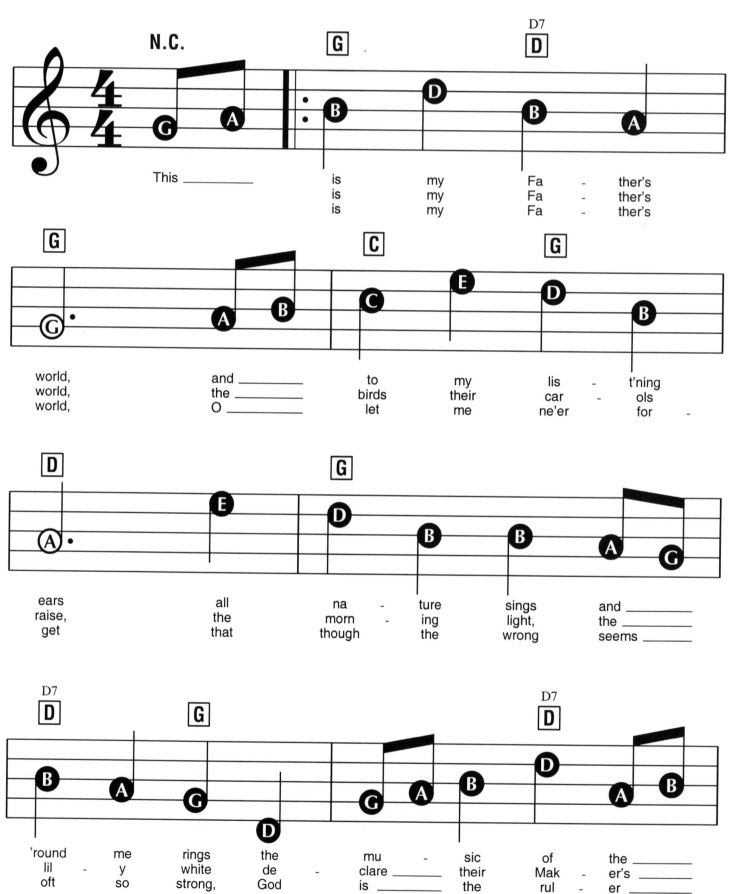

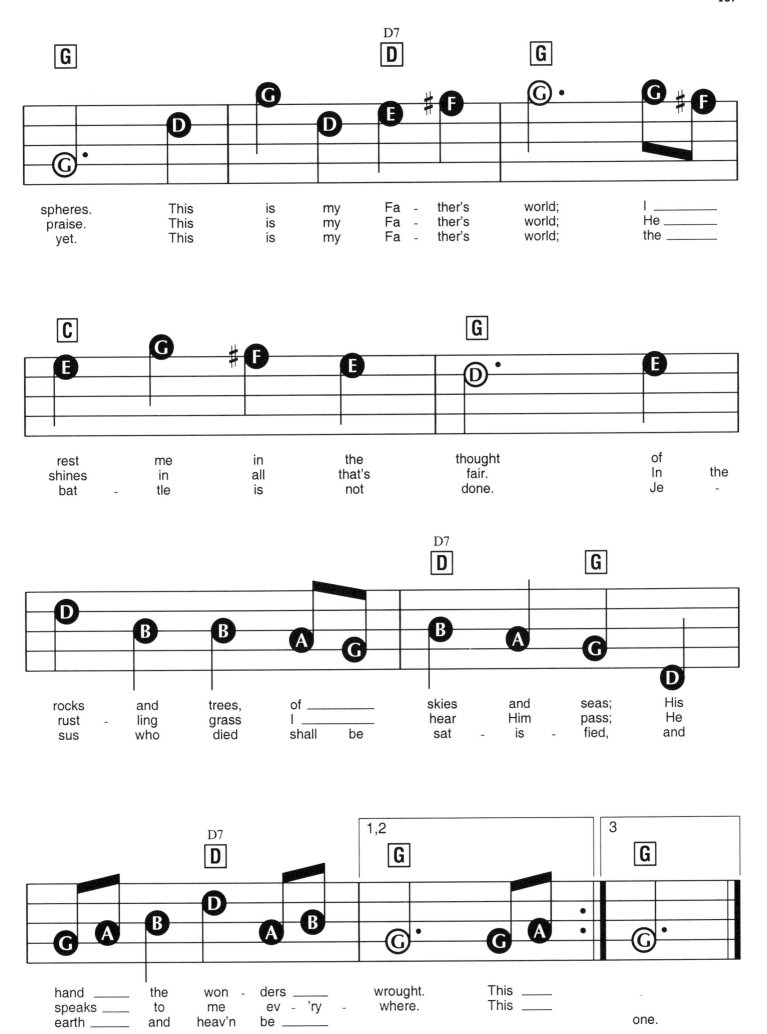

This Little Light of Mine

Registration 4
Rhythm: Fox Trot or Swing

African-American Spiritual

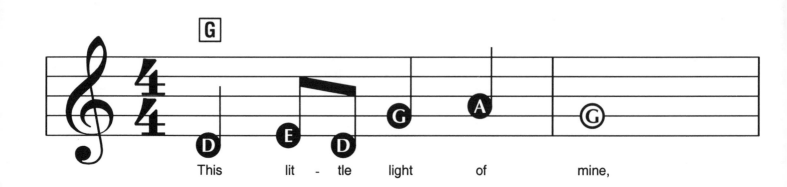

This lit - tle light of mine,

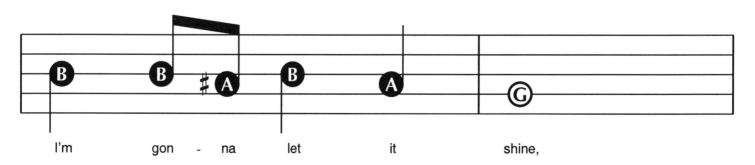

I'm gon - na let it shine,

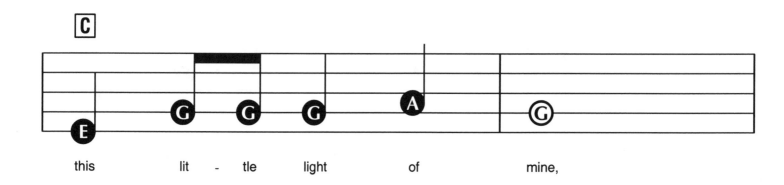

this lit - tle light of mine,

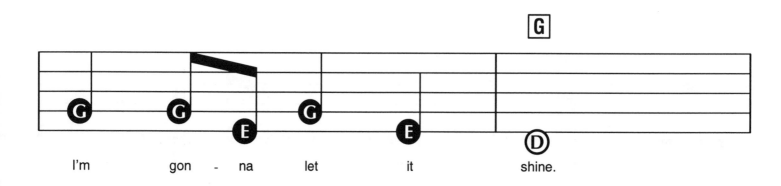

I'm gon - na let it shine.

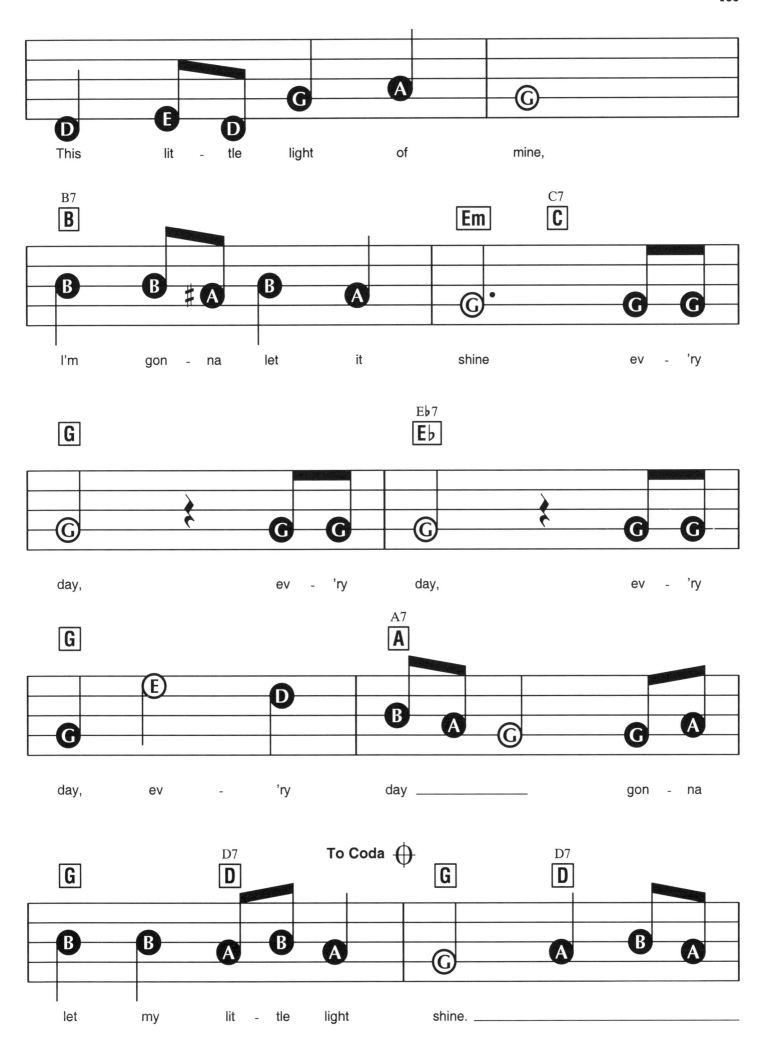

110

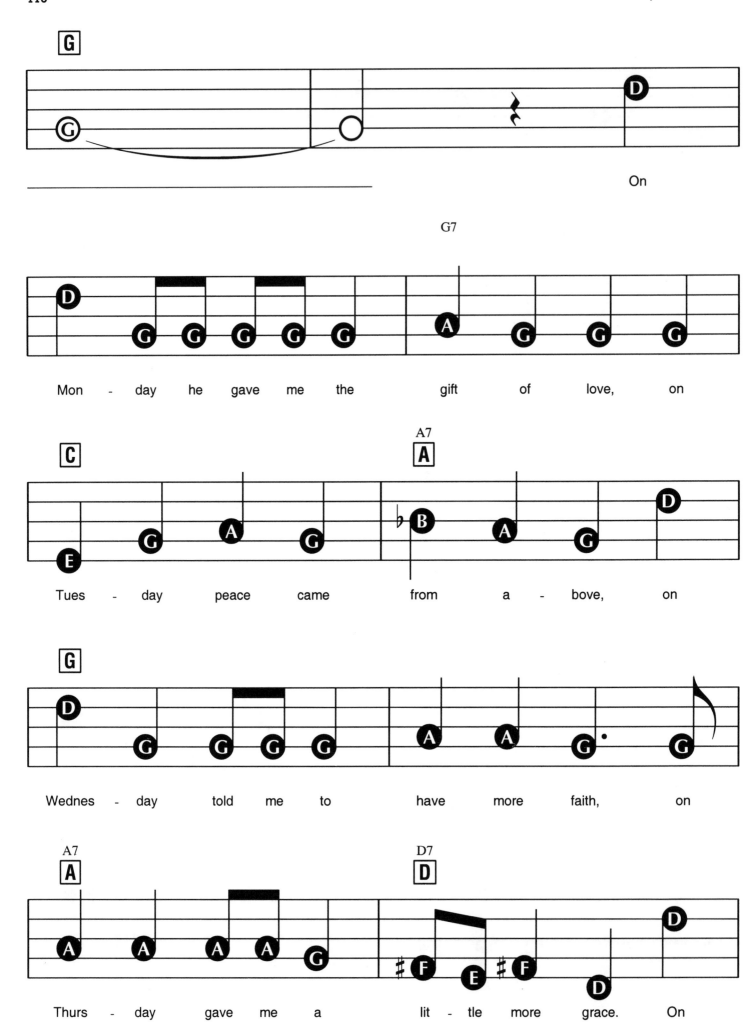

G

G7

D G G G G A G G G

Fri - day told me to watch and pray, on

C

A7
A

E E G A G A B A G G

Sat - ur - day told me just what to say, on

G

B7
B

Em

A7
A

B B B B B B B B G G A

Sun - day gave me the pow - er di - vine, just to

D.C. al Coda
(Return to beginning
Play to ⊕ and
Skip to Coda)

G

D7
D

G

B B A B A G

let my lit - tle light shine.

CODA
⊕

G

D7
D

G

G A B A G

shine. _____

This Little Light of Mine

(2nd Tune)

Registration 8
Rhythm: Country or Fox Trot

Traditional

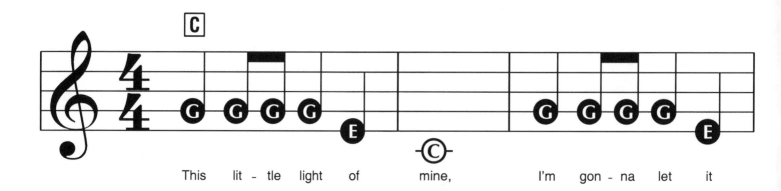

This lit - tle light of mine, I'm gon - na let it

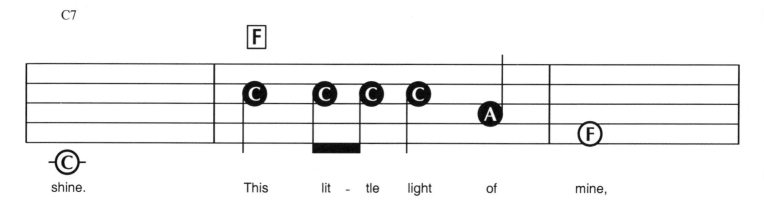

C7

shine. This lit - tle light of mine,

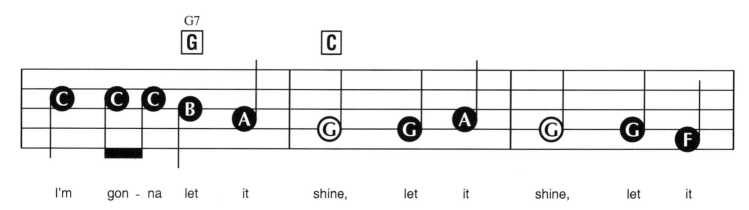

G7

I'm gon - na let it shine, let it shine, let it

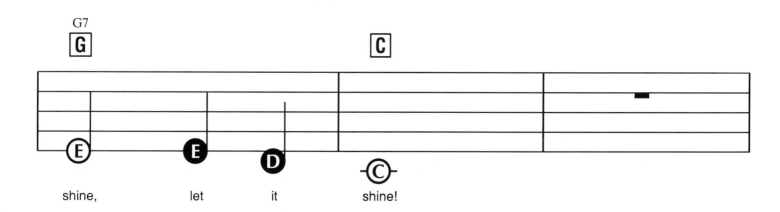

G7

shine, let it shine!

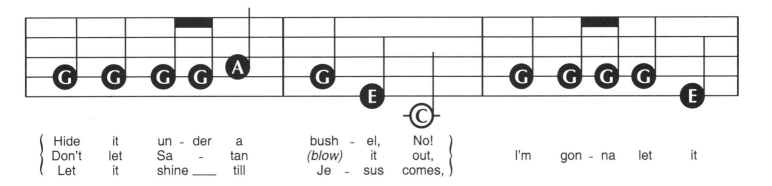

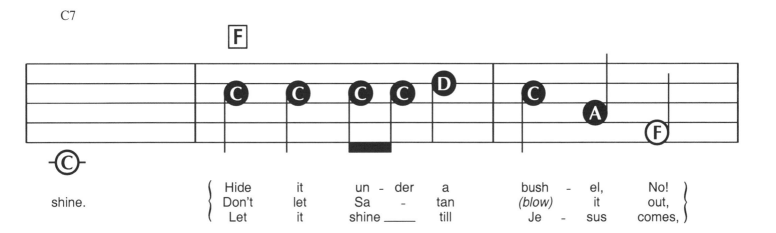

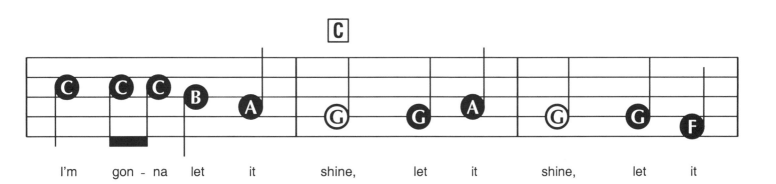

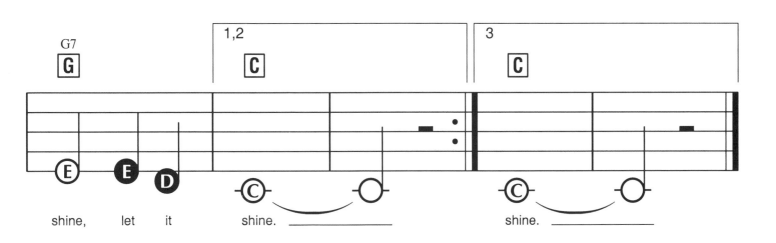

Thy Word Have I Hid in My Heart

Registration 1
Rhythm: Waltz

Text based on Psalm 119:11
Music by Earnest O. Sellers

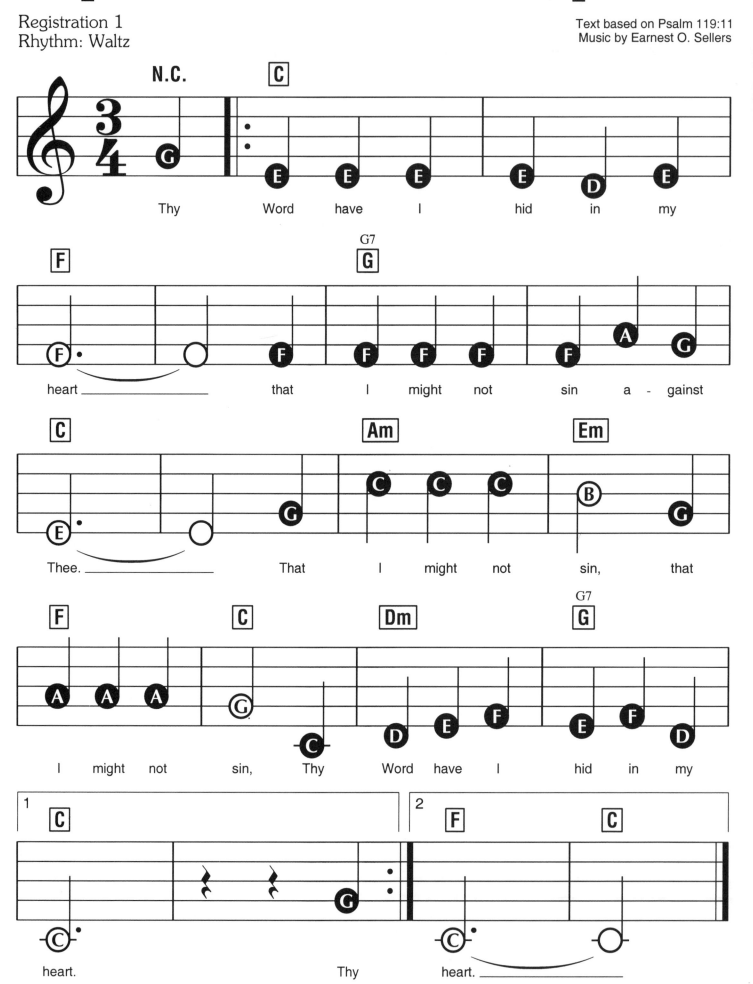

What a Mighty God We Serve

Registration 4
Rhythm: Fox Trot or Country

Traditional

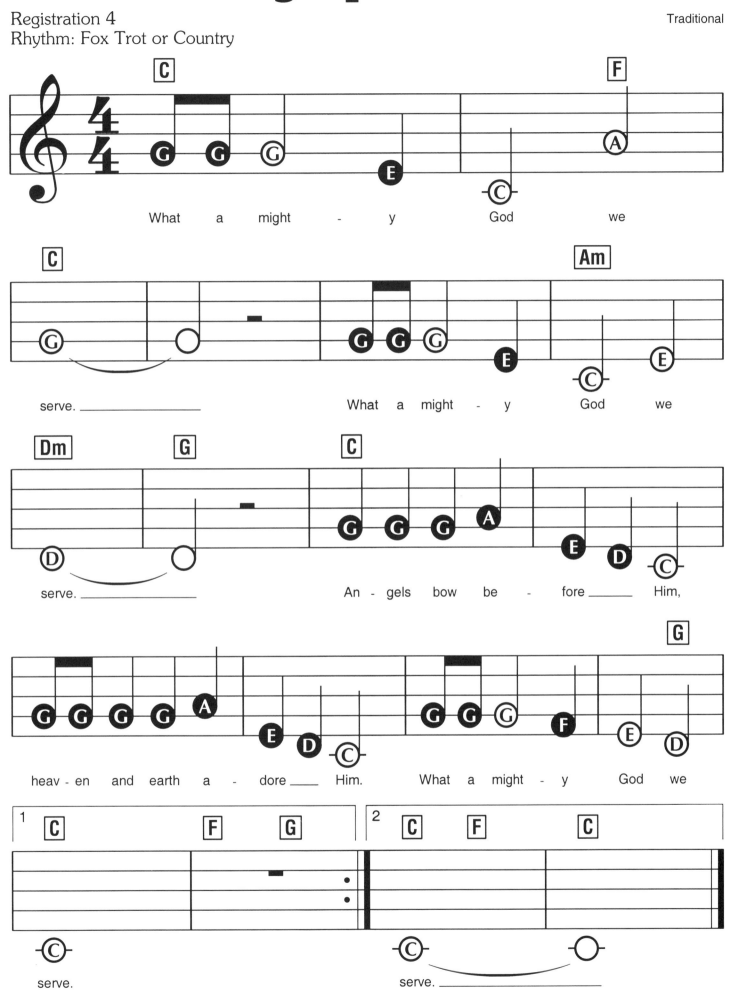

The Wise Man and the Foolish Man

Registration 8
Rhythm: Country or Swing

Traditional

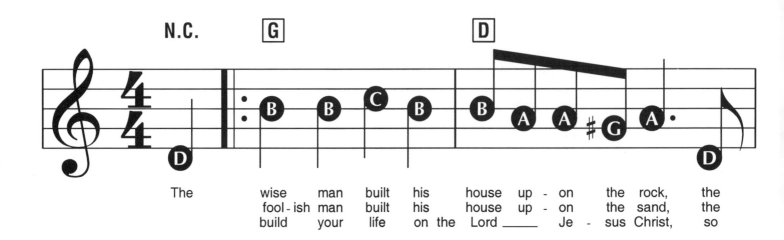

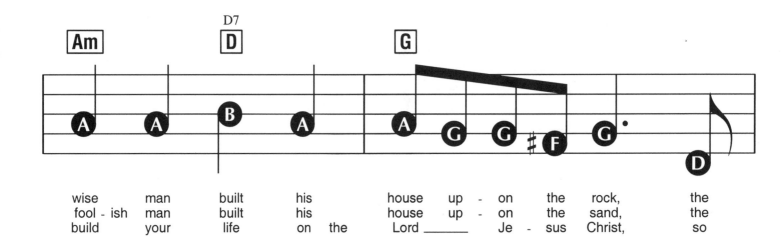

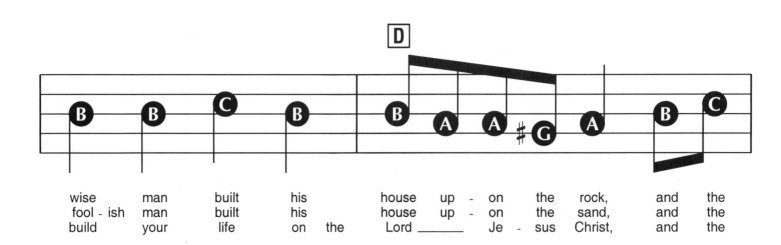

117

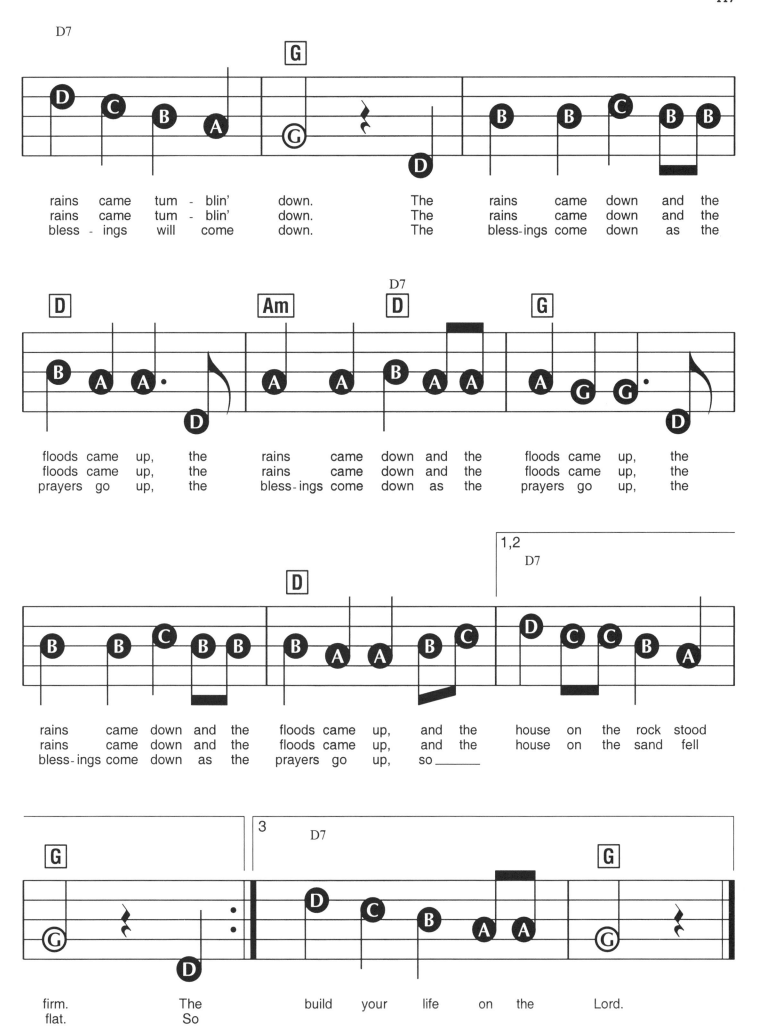

Zacchaeus

Registration 8
Rhythm: Fox Trot

Traditional

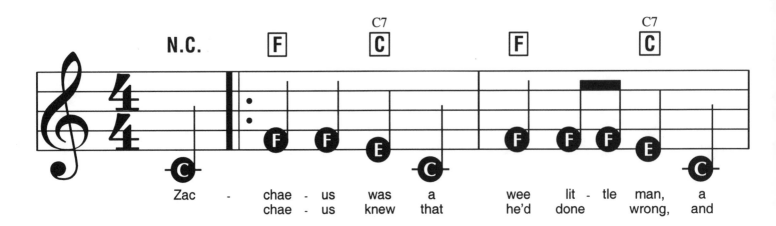

Zac - chae - us was a wee lit - tle man, a
chae - us knew that he'd done wrong, and

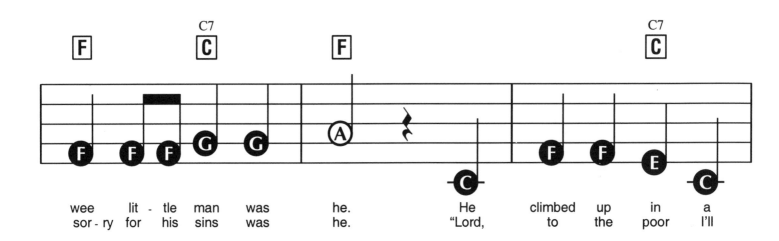

wee lit - tle man was he. He climbed up in a
sor - ry for his sins was he. "Lord, to the poor I'll

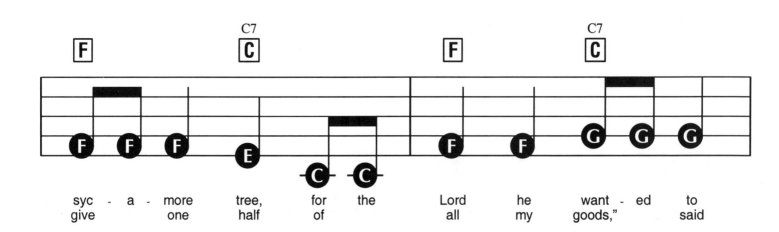

syc - a - more tree, for the Lord he want - ed to
give one half of all my goods," said

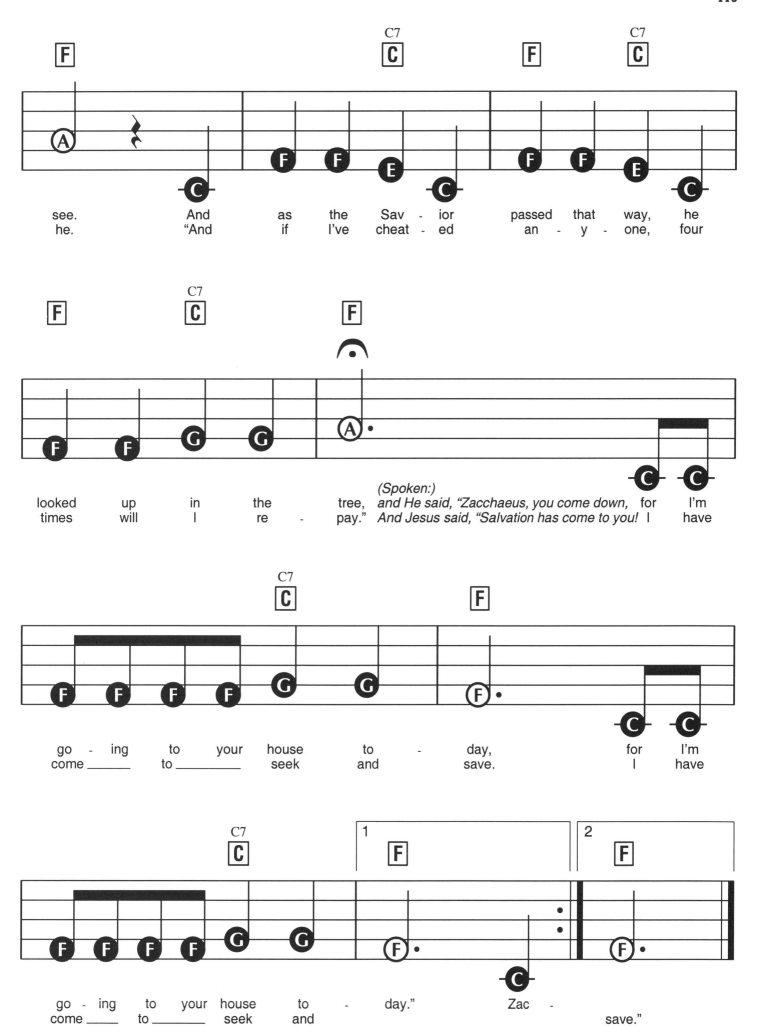

When the Saints Go Marching In

Registration 2
Rhythm: Swing

Words by Katherine E. Purvis
Music by James M. Black

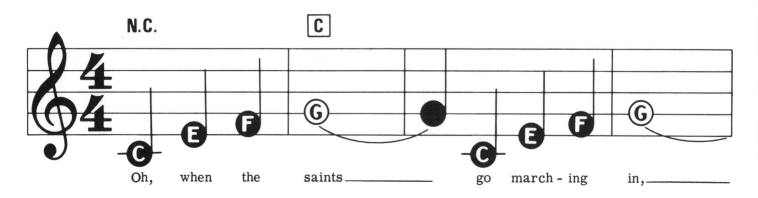

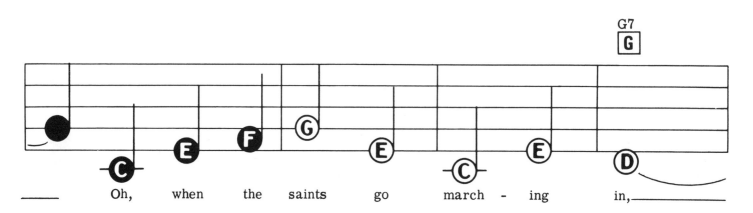

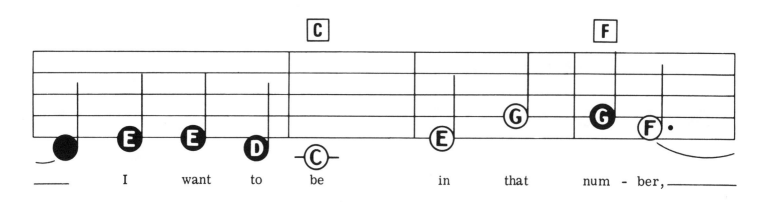

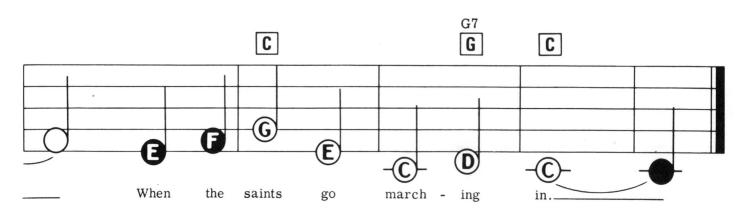